How to Get Speaking Gigs Fast!

The Ultimate Formula to Getting Paid

Barry Schimmel

Loren Michaels Harris

www.Howtogetspeakinggigsfast.com

How to get speaking gigs fast strategy:

- Free One-On-One Consultation
  Spend 20-30 minutes working together to
  create a plan for getting speaking gigs fast
- Everyone who applies for a consultation
  receives a gift

4 WAYS TO REGISTER

Mobile Text
Text to: 58885 your name and email with the
keyword **Formula**

Voice
Call 866-603-3995 PIN # 146968

Web
www.bonus.howtogetspeakinggigsfast.com

QR Code

Table of Contents

Dedication

Barry ~

This book is dedicated to…

My parents, Burt Schimmel and Sue Hardman, whose guidance throughout my life was everything that was needed. They taught me to work hard, be honest, and follow my dreams.

My wife of twenty years, Jennifer, has always been an inspiration to me and to our two children. She has not only helped me write 7 books but always supported my efforts, making each journey purposeful.

My son Alec who is ready to leave home and start a new chapter in his life as a college student. He has made me so proud as a father and a friend. I love him dearly.

My daughter Elissa is a true leader in every sense of the word. She will be starting college this year. I am grateful for every moment we spend together and looking forward to her next chapter. My love for her couldn't be greater. Proud daddy!

Thank you to all my clients for believing in me and making this possible. They stood by me during all my learning moments and I wish each of them the happiness and success they desire.

Loren ~

Having the privilege to share my story, to speak to the truths that have enabled me to do what I have always dreamed of doing, is due to so many that I encountered along my journey. I would need to write thousands of books to have the space to thank everyone who is responsible for where I am today. I must of course begin somewhere, so I thank each person that crossed my path in the 22 foster homes I passed through over the years of my childhood. I thank both my adoptive and biological families for their collective contributions to my life of yesterday and today. I am so very grateful to Barry and Jennifer Schimmel for seeing and believing in me and my message.

Most of all, I thank God for Dr. Brian L. Rzepczynski. Thank you, Brian, for providing me my first book on how to become a speaker and for pushing me directly into my purpose in this life. You have provided me a level of joy and happiness that until you, I never knew was even possible.

Loren Michaels Harris

Introduction

What strategy will help you get speaking gigs fast?

Before we begin, let us tell you why we titled this book How to Get Speaking Gigs Fast:

- Digital Tools: You will learn how to use digital platforms to find speaking opportunities fast.
- The economy has shifted, communication has changed, and we "the people" have changed; therefore, you cannot run your businesses, and your speaking strategy, as if it were still the year 2000.
- Dollars: You must make money or you're a hobby. You must have money to pay your bills. The more money you have the more people you can help.

The aim of this book is to provide you with a proven and repeatable method for finding new gigs fast. It is our desire to convey a clear and simple step-by-step process for understanding and strategically implementing these proven tactics, with the result of achieving unstoppable growth.

The underlying belief behind this book is:

The world is changing.

If you don't believe this simple premise, if you want to run your business as if an extraordinary revolution is not taking place, then this book is not for you. We are writing for the person who realizes that things are different, but who wants to succeed anyway.

Our promise is that this current revolution is not a death sentence for your business. The savvy marketer (and we are all marketers) who understands the demands being placed on current businesses can beat the odds and realize massive growth.

In the pages to come, we will help you change your mindset on what's possible and provide you with actionable resources to grow your speaking business fast. What we truly aim to do is facilitate your personal growth and leverage the opportunities in our changing world.

Barry's Story

I grew up with a loving family in a tough intercity neighborhood of Chicago. Funds were tight, and violence could easily be found. It taught me to be mentally and physically strong. It also taught me a solid work ethic. I knew that if I wanted something, I needed to work for it and I did. Cutting grasses, delivering newspapers, you name it, I did it. By the time I was in high school, I was helping my parents pay the mortgage. It really was about survival.

As soon as I graduated high school, I joined the Air Force and was eventually stationed in Germany as an SP. I had the honor to protecting the American hostages when they were released from Iran back in 1981. The Air Force taught me so much and I am proud to have served my country. The Air Force also gave me a path to get my college education. Once I was discharged, I worked full-time and was a full-time student. After receiving my bachelor's degree, I continued and received my MBA through Roosevelt University.

Education, hard work, and a commitment to helping myself and others has been the theme of my entire life. For the last 25 years, I have successfully incorporated my strengths into the marketing and technology industries, building 3 multi-million-dollar companies. Now, I work with others who have a mission and passion to continue to advance themselves, to contribute to others, and to leave a positive impact on the world.

Loren's Story

Loren Michaels Harris, a survivor of the foster care system and an adoptee, strives to share the combined learnings of his time within the foster care system and his life experiences with those seeking insight into how to accomplish the most out of their lives.

Loren specializes in working with middle school through high school youth and correctional systems, but the depth and variety of his topics resonate with a much broader audience. He draws upon his upbringing, which includes 22 mothers in total, and his original music to motivate and inspire others in overcoming their obstacles to success and achieving the life they want flexible solutions for your needs.

Loren has spoken across a broad spectrum of industries and organizations as well as multiple media channels. Engagements include schools, speaker associations, and large corporations such as Whirlpool.

Our Vision

Loren engaged Barry to help him expand his speaking business in 2016. As a professional speaker, Barry was able to share effective tools and strategies that Loren saw almost immediate results with. Loren is an action taker and takes ownership of fully implementing what he learns. He then expands upon it to achieve profound results.

Through working with each other, we found that we both have a passion for partnering with others to help them achieve their goals. On top of that, there is a dynamic synergy when we bring together our areas of expertise.

Visionaries by nature, we knew that we had to expand our level of contribution and influence to help more people. Barry's expertise in marketing and technology combined with Loren's deep understanding of how to connect with people and the psychology of meeting peoples' needs, led to the development of *How to Get Speaking Gigs Fast* – the book, our interactive workshops, and our coaching programs.

Collaborating with our unique strengths has delivered to our community a renewed sense of purpose and specific action items that lead to success. What we are witnessing is people who were stalled having momentum; those that couldn't get a call back, now are being sought out; and those that thought that speaking wasn't a viable revenue stream, now have a growing business.

As you read this book, we encourage you to open your mind to new ideas, strategies, and tactics. Push past limiting beliefs, be courageous in trying new methods, and remember that you are here to serve.

To achieving your purpose,

Barry Schimmel & Loren Michaels Harris

Part 1: Marketing Insights

The following section will provide an overview of key insights Barry has gained with his years in marketing and technology. Why is marketing mentioned here? Because you are marketing yourself to event planners, business leaders, audiences, etc. A general foundational base of knowledge is beneficial to positioning yourself as a speaker people want to hire.

Some background on Barry:
Before opening my marketing company—Microshare Intl—in 2010, I had grown three multi-million-dollar businesses. Prior to that, I received traditional training while earning my MBA from Roosevelt University in Chicago, IL.

While running my companies, I always knew that it was crucial to keep my finger on the pulse of my marketing. After 25 years, I've learned what works and what doesn't.

In that journey, I had to have clarity and continually stay current with new trends and insights. I learned from the most effective and cutting-edge marketers, and I executed countless sales and marketing campaigns.

This section is a glimpse of a myriad of books read; dozens of trainings, seminars, masterminds and coaching programs; and thousands of mistakes.

Chapter 1: Changing Your Mindset

It is essential to change your mindset in order to change your life.

Myth:
Mindset takes a long time to change, and the longer you have had a belief the more time it takes to revise it. This outdated view goes back to the early days of psychology and neuroscience, when scientists told us erroneously that our brains are hardwired, static and fixed like some sort of machine made purely of physical parts.

What is Mindset?

A set of assumptions, methods, or notations held by one or more people or groups of people that is so established that it creates a powerful incentive within these people or groups to continue to adopt or accept prior behaviors, choices, or tools.

Barry's Perspective:
Let me clearly explain why mindset is so important. I hear all the time how entrepreneurs are struggling and digital marketing doesn't work. The biggest complaint I hear is, "I have been burned so many times I don't trust anyone."

I can't argue with them because that is their experience. I can help them change their mindset when they follow a proven, systematic approach which delivers results.

With this foundational understanding in place, you must evaluate where you are now and where you intend to be a year from now (or even 5 years from now).

How to change your mindset

1. Gather information about your best clients to understand what problems you solve for them, and who they are. Also, find out what they love and hate and why they love and why they hate.

2. Analyze how your competition is converting new leads. The foundation of getting leads is optimizing your message so prospects can understand what problem you solve and your solutions.

3. Examine your beliefs about what you are doing and how you are doing it. You must identify what's not working so you can stop doing it and focus on what others are doing that is working effectively.

4. Create your vision with a clear set of goals which will shape your mindset to get the results you desire.

5. Create a message that is clear, concise and consistent throughout all your platforms.

6. Protect your mindset against the naysayers and people who want to drag you down. You also must protect it against poor information and against overload. Keeping your confidence is essential. So please stay on the right path, look to improve yourself and to help others along the way.

The truth about mindset

In my marketing firm, Microshare Intl, I have seen many businesses grow substantially—in influence and revenue—and it always started with changing the mindset of the business owner/entrepreneur. On the flip-side, we have also seen numerous companies fail because they were unwilling to change or did not believe in the new ways to do things. "The difference between success and failure was always in mindset".

Successful entrepreneurs can change their mindset, and in turn, influence their marketing and sales activities; unsuccessful ones don't. This is true in every industry.

Change the World & Make Money?

In my experience, all businesses (even the solo entrepreneurs) function for two reasons:
1. To fulfill a mission (think Mission Statement)
2. To generate revenues

Most companies try to accomplish both, but in varying degrees. As a generalization, not-for-profit organizations lean towards trying to fulfill a Mission, where small and medium size companies (which include Authors, Speakers and Entrepreneurs) focus on revenues.

Here are some great questions that I love to ask my marketing clients, and sadly most of them don't have answer for them:

- What do you love about your business?
- What legacy do you want to leave?
- What have you done in the past toward that legacy?
- What is your company's Higher Purpose? (For example, the online shoe store Zappos says, "We are all part of something great... To put a smile upon your face.")

Your mindset is essential to your success. If you believe "nothing will work for you," your actions will align to that and it is exactly what you will get. If you believe that life is always changing and that you need to be open to learning (both via success and failure for yourself and what you see with others), the opportunities are endless for you.

In addition, remember that what you do is always about other people. If you don't believe that, you need to re-frame the way you think about your purpose. You must come from a desire to help people. Now this doesn't mean you don't get paid. There is a fair exchange in value but having the mindset to provide solutions to peoples' needs changes everything from the words you use to the conversations you have. This applies to the deals you close as well.

Embrace the power you have in you. Learn, grow, and then learn some more. Commit to your goals and act on what leads to success. For so many people, it's not who you think you are that holds you back — it's who you think you're not.

Mindset Case Study

Dawn Pruchniak, a Family Affairs Specialist, was looking to expand her successful business. As part of our strategy development, Barry worked with her 1:1 and worked through the six steps to help her align her mindset to her goals. During this time, Dr. Kris had some profound "aha" moments.

She realized:
- Who she loved to work with
- Who she didn't want to work with
- What she loved to do and where her passion was

Speak to Sell

Together, we worked to solidify her unique value proposition and started communicating her unique story to the audience she was looking to attract. She embraced focusing and conveying what set her apart from all the other specialists.

In the end, Dawn decided to market her book "The Best Gift is Your Last Gift" and it became a #1 Best Seller on Amazon.

She is speaking around the country to educate her audience on the benefits of having their affairs in order. This is how she positions herself as an expert and offers her online products and services.

Tactically, we built a graphical framework to illustrate her services and define exactly what problems she solves and get patients faster. The foundation of the framework follows this illustration:

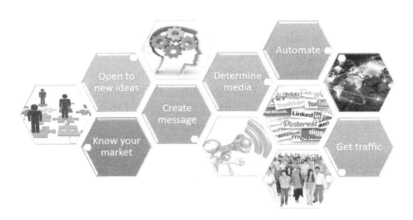

In addition, we helped her create a clear, concise message so we could target the speaking opportunities she desired.

This is where speaking came into the equation. understanding who she wanted to speak to and the unique problem she would help to solve.

Dawn's has an online program www.TheBestGiftisYourLastGift.com and has regular online webinars and has a full schedule of speaking opportunities. Learn more at www.DawnPruchniak.com Great things that happen when you have an open mind and you act.

Chapter 2: Everything Has A Beginning

From our favorite bedtime stories; "Once Upon A Time", to The Bible; "In the beginning", every story has a beginning and the same is true for each message which is intended to be shared within the universe.

Finding the beginning of many things in life can prove to be more difficult than ever imagined once one begins to search for where something all began. In the case of my message for instance, for many years I thought that my story; that part of me that was so different from most other people, that thing that caused people to stare in disbelief when hearing about it, began the day my adoptive mother died suddenly when I was a child. It was not until I located my birth mother at age 32 that I began to reconsider the starting line of my race, otherwise known as life, as actually beginning the moment of my conception. I now know that many of our messages, messages intended to reach the masses eventually, in many cases began being constructed long before any of us were even aware that there was a message, let alone one that we would one day be responsible for sharing with the world.

Of course, it is my opinion, but I truly believe that the reason so many in this world depart this world never having shared their unique message with the masses, is that most of those people were never able to find where it was that their message began.

I remember for many years I truly thought that my primary objective in life was to do whatever was required to reach that level of success or that pinnacle of achievement, wherein I could plant my flag, declare my self-worth, and now begin writing my story. I spent countless days, months, and years…attempting in vain to cover my tracks from a past that I no more had control over covering, than I had in the creation of.

I, for many years, unknowingly dug myself deeper into a hole of regret simply because I was aimlessly seeking outside validation that I was worthy of even the most basic human respects. Having found out several days after burying my adoptive mother, that I was not legally adopted, that I actually possessed a name different than the one I had known my entire life, and that I would no longer be able to reside in the place I had always known as home…was the beginning of my understanding that things for me were not as they seemed, nor had they ever been. Before I could wrap my mind around these new realizations regarding my very existence, my story began yet another chapter, the chapter that would span over 6 years and be written between the thresholds of 22 different foster homes.

I have always possessed a passion for reading autobiographies, I was drawn to autobiographies because #1: they were truth and not fiction, and #2: because they were written by the very person who lived the story. I found myself further intrigued by the fact that anyone who has written an autobiography that is on the shelf of a library or bookstore, well…they must have done something worthy of being shared, right?

My perspective on autobiographical material in the 1970's was much different than it is today, with the abundant world of self-publishing and eBooks the way it is, one can never truly know if a story or message is truth or fiction.

The very first memory I have of thinking that perhaps one day I would like to share my life's story, that maybe... just maybe, someone somewhere would find what I have to say helpful or interesting was at age 26. I was in the throes of what I still to this day refer as "a magical time" in my life.

I had been severely depressed, so much so, that I was borderline suicidal. I was doing an internship at a #1 Urban radio station in Hollywood, California, and was the manager of the apartment complex I resided within in the Hollywood Hills. On the outside, it would appear that for a 25-year-old in Hollywood of 1987, I did not have it so bad, especially as there were many young people in Hollywood my age that were not doing as well as I. Each day, it was not uncommon for me to see kids my age sleeping on the sidewalks and in the alleyways of downtown Hollywood. I saw many of my peers, kids who had come to Hollywood in search of the very same things I had, slip deeper and deeper into drugs and prostitution simply to survive.

Here I was nonetheless, living in a beautiful apartment, rent free, utility free, and a decent salary on top of it all, yet in still I was battling depression on a near daily basis. My position at the radio station allowed me access to the station anytime day or night, and since it was a few short blocks from my apartment, I found myself spending hours there, listening to the music and practicing my "on air" personality in preparation of the day when they would finally allow me to open the mic and say even one word.

Even with what would appear to have been (outwardly at least), a pretty decent lifestyle for a young person competing in the competition capital of the world, Hollywood, California…I could not beat the never-ending cycle of depression and began to seriously fear I might take my own life. I decided to reach out for some help but had no idea where to look or whom to ask so I began looking in the newspapers.

At the time, I was using my voice primarily to carve my niche in the world of those seeking stardom, I did voiceover work, jingle sang on the side, and for a while even hosted Karaoke night at a local sushi bar. Each week I would hit the corner 7/11 to stand around and copy auditions for the upcoming week from one of their copies of "Drama Log", a weekly publication somewhat like "Variety" where actors, dancers, and singers alike, would pray their big break would emerge from.

This particular week it was not an audition notification that would change the course of my life forever, it would be a tiny advertisement for "Hypnotherapy"! In the far-right corner of one of the pages, the smallest ad on the page…is where I saw it. The ad promised to help you do everything from lose weight, stop smoking, or get past any challenge or hurdle that might be stopping you from achieving your dreams in life. I quickly copied the telephone number and promised myself that I would call as soon as I made it back to my apartment.

I did end up calling, but it took me over a week to gather up the courage to do so. I made the appointment for the next day to meet the therapist; Anne…at her home in Studio City…otherwise known to those of us in Hollywood as; The Valley.

Over the course of the next several weeks, I experienced everything from nightmares to insomnia…binge eating to no appetite at all. Anne had explained to me prior to beginning our sessions that these things might all happen, but not to fear because once we make it through those not so pleasant times, then the wonderful things would take place! My nightmares would now be replaced by cognitive dreams, is what Anne promised…and for some reason, I believed her.

When Anne would count me under to begin my hypnosis session, she would routinely ask me to envision myself in PEOPLE Magazine as I ascended the stairway she always had me construct within my mind. Anne would instruct me to pick the PEOPLE Magazine up, feel the weight of it, flip through the pages, etc. I followed this pattern of "going under" each of the 6 times I met with Anne.

One week stands out for me in my sessions with Anne, it was to be my final week of treatment, but the beginning of a friendship that would last many years. Unbeknownst to me, the week prior to my final week Anne had planted a trigger word within my mind, a word that upon my arrival to our session, Anne need only speak the word and I would begin the grieving process that Anne was convinced I had never experienced as a child, the process that she believed would release me from much of the inner turmoil that led me to feelings of inadequacy, low self-esteem, and virtually no self-worth.

I could not have been in Anne's living room for more than 5 minutes before she dropped the trigger word and all hell broke loose! I shall never forget that the word she used was "chocolate chip cookie". One minute we were chatting about how my week had been since our last session, and then Anne nonchalantly asked me if I would like a "chocolate chip cookie". I began to feel a combination of tears, pain, heartbreak, regret, sadness, betrayal, and what felt like several hundred other emotions begin to boil up within me. I moved throughout the living room half pacing like a caged animal would, half feeling as if I might need to run as fast as I possibly could due to my clothing being on fire.

I remember clearly that I could not stop my vocal chords from producing the words WHY…WHY…WHY? I tried to ask other questions with my eyes to Anne, but they too would not cooperate. Both my hands had converted themselves from flesh and bone into what now felt like two solid steel balls worthlessly hanging from the ends of my arms. Finally, I could take no more and simply collapsed onto the floor.

I awoke still on the floor, but now my head was in Anne's lap, there was a quilt thrown over me. Anne was gently caressing my forehead with what felt like a cold wash cloth, and her body was slowly rocking me back and forth. I attempted to turn my eyes up at Anne to see what she was doing, but quickly realized that not only did my eyes burn badly, but they were swollen shut from the 3 ½ straight hours of crying, of grieving…that Anne said that I had experienced.

I left Anne's house a different man that day, for it was only 4 days later that I awoke from having what Anne had promised I would have eventually…my very first cognitive dream. I had dreamed I was in the studio audience of a game show entitled "Apology Accepted", the host was Chuck Woolery from "Love Connection". This game was like Love Connection except we the audience did not vote on dates for the contestant, we voted on which of three apologies would be the perfect apology to repair the damaged relationship between the contestant and someone else. I sat through the entire show and then came the time in which we were asked to exit the theater. There were what were called pages at the game shows back then, and the one at the end of my row was stretching out their arm for us to pass by and find the exit. It was at that moment that I spoke aloud to no one in particular…" what a great idea for a business…who came up with this idea?" Every single person in the theater looked at me and in one collective voice they said; "No one Loren, this is for you…IF you want it!"

I immediately awoke and ran to my dining room table. Being that I was an apartment complex manager, I kept a stack of 3x5 index cards beside the telephone, along with a cup of #10 pencils, to take down maintenance calls and complaints from the tenants. When picking up the pencil, it was truly my intention to only jot down the name "Apology Accepted", but as I reached for the 3x5 card, my eye caught the copy of PEOPLE Magazine that I had inadvertently began purchasing, perhaps due to Anne's subliminal implanting the whole "see yourself in PEOPLE Magazine" thing.

I never even gave it a second thought, I simply flipped through the pages until I found the masthead, located the name of the editor of PEOPLE Magazine, wrote his name on the front of the card followed by the address (which I still remember to this day as being on Avenue of the Americas). I then flipped the card over and wrote in pencil…" I just awoke from a dream, I am about to create a company called APOLOGY ACCEPTED, I am going to do apologies for anyone who can't for whatever reason…say "I'm sorry" for themselves! Please call me".

I placed a 10-cent stamp on that 3x5 card written in pencil and mailed it off to New York City from Hollywood…One week to the day the editor of PEOPLE Magazine himself called me. One thing led to another, and before it was all said and done, I found myself with a 3-page feature article within PEOPLE's bestselling issue of the year: The Worst and Best Dressed Issue of December 12, 1988. Little did I know when I sent my message to NYC written on nothing more than a 3x5 card in pencil, that this small and seemingly bizarre message would be my first opportunity to experience what it feels like to be the one person chosen by the creator to usher something into this world that this world has never seen before. This for me was the beginning of my story…at the time, but things were about to become even more bizarre, something I would quickly grow to understand is how it is and should always feel when one is creating their very own never-ending story.

Market, Message, Media

"Without a solid foundation, you'll have trouble creating anything of value." ~ Erica Oppenheimer

Target Market:
The market a company wants to sell its products and services to. This encompasses a targeted set of customers to whom it directs its marketing efforts towards. A target market can be differentiated from the market (as a whole) by geography, buying power/household income, demographics, and much more.

When you are competing for a speaking gig as well as working your business, you need to be aware and incorporate marketing strategies. You are selling YOU – your products, your services, your expertise, your results, etc. As such, we will briefly go through some marketing principles that you should consciously integrate into what you do.

So, the question to you is where you start:

- Market?
- Message?
- Media?

Where Do You Start?

Whenever I ask an entrepreneur or business team where they start their marketing strategy, 95% of the responses are incorrectly:

- 85% answer with Message
- 10% answer with Media

The most important element for any successful marketing campaign is understanding who you are selling to and what problem are you solving. Which leaves Market as the correct answer.

Part of understanding the market and how best to campaign involves gather information from your best client, as well as analyzing your competition.

Good communication skills are at the cornerstone of creating results since so much of your relationship with your client has to do with what you communicate, and not just what you do behind the scenes.

Listening is an art, after all, and not everyone knows how to do it properly. If you can master the art of listening, you'll improve your relationships by connecting with a deeper level of understanding.

Remember, your clients and audience care about the problem you are solving for them and will even share other problems they have that you might be able to solve. Keep the communication lines open, but focus on the right questions.

Market

Your upfront research in defining your target audience/market will save you time, money, and reduce your stress. Knowing your target audience is the first step to achieving the success you desire.

Factors to consider include:

- **Who are you selling to?**
  Demographics: Gender, education, profession, income, home ownership, geographic location, family, lifestyle, online activity, ideal qualities, and nightmare qualities?

- **What makes them want to buy?**
  Psychographics: Their wants, their innermost fears and frustrations, their objections to buying, and what would make them buy.

- **Do they have money?**
  Another big mistake I see with companies and entrepreneurs that are failing is spending their time and marketing dollars on a target audience that doesn't have the ability to pay for their product and services.

Message

Message is a verbal, written, or recorded communication sent to or left for a recipient who cannot be contacted directly. Your message should be directed at your target audience while solving one problem at a time.

Ask yourself:

- How will my message bring in new clients?
- How can my message increase conversions?
- How can my message increase the amount I sell to my current clients?
- How can my message help my clients?

- How can my message increase my authority?
- How can my message support my 5-star reputation?
- How will my message integrate with my marketing automation?

Steps to creating your marketing message

Creating your Message:
1. Know your market
2. Identify problems
3. Present your solution
4. Present results (posted from current clients for credibility)
5. Explain what makes you different

We have already identified our target market and the problems they have. The next step is to present your product or service as a simple solution to fix their problem.

Continuing the process, the next step is to present the results you've produced for other clients in the same situation. It's not enough just to tell people you have a solution; you must prove to them that your solution works. Realize, you can talk all day about how you solved this and that problem, but people are skeptical and won't automatically believe you.

People will believe other people who are like them that have achieved positive results. In this step, you'll need to prove your results by providing testimonials from current and former customers as well as case studies of actual problems that were solved and the results that were achieved.

Therefore, your message, has two functions:

- To leave a great first impression
- And to move prospects through the sales cycle

Last, you must explain what makes you different from your competitors. You need to communicate your uniqueness!

Prospects are looking for you to communicate your differences. And those differences need to have perceived value to the prospect. It needs to be something relevant and what they care about.

The Big Marketing Message Mistake

The biggest marketing message mistake that companies make is communicating "What-We-Do" instead of "What's-In-It-For-Me." If these were two radio channels (i.e. WWD vs. WIIFM), which one do you think your prospect would rather hear?
While you are transmitting on WWD, your prospect is looking for the WIIFM station. In order for your message to match your market, you need to be broadcasting on WIIFM.

For a video that will guide you through Creating a Message That Gets Results, sign-up at www.digitaltodollars.net.

Media

Media is the means of communication -radio and television, newspapers, magazines, and the Internet - that reach or influence people widely:

There are 3 types of media

- **Paid Media**
  Paid media is what most people think of when they think of advertising. It's the most traditional of the three types of digital media— you pay to leverage an existing channel. Examples include digital display ads, paid search, and native advertising. Paid media lets you reach a large-scale audience and direct attention to your content to those that wouldn't otherwise find it. For example, if you don't rank on the first page of Google for an important keyword, buying an AdWords ad for that keyword will get you views that you couldn't get organically. The downside of paid media is that audiences are bombarded with ads in almost every sphere of their lives and seeing another ad might not elicit a strong response from them. But if used correctly, it can be a great way to draw in new customers to your content. The goal of using paid media is for the value of this access to dramatically outweigh the cost in dollars of the ad or promotion.

- **Earned Media**
  Earned media is often referred to as "online word of mouth." It includes SEO rankings, social media mentions, and content getting picked up by a third party. In effect, your

customers become your promotion channel. Earned media is free, acquired by good strategic practices on social media and SEO, as well as good PR practices. You can't buy someone's good opinion online, which is why this is known as "earned" media—you must work for it. It can be immensely effective because of its organic nature. It's also more credible than a paid ad—more people will listen to a real person's endorsement. Earned media can be problematic because you don't control it, and sometimes your stakeholders have negative opinions of your service. However, word of mouth is a key sales driver, so cultivating earned media is extremely worthwhile. How can my message increase the amount I sell to my prospects and current clients?

- **Owned Media**
  Owned media is perhaps the least understood of the three types of digital media. It's any media that is controlled directly by your brand, such as your company website, blog, or social media account. Everything that you publish on this channel is yours, and you can adapt or change content as you need. Promoting your company on your Twitter account costs far less than promoting it with an AdWords ad.

  Owned media builds off your existing relationships with customers as well as drawing in prospects who are further along in the decision-making process. When your audience interacts with your owned media properties, they're often drawn to explore more of your content—if someone likes a blog post on your website, he might click around and view your company capabilities.

Owned media also has the benefit of longevity. Advertisements will only run for so long, but your website will continue to draw in customers as long as it's active and updated. The downside is that there are no guarantees. You could be creating high-quality, well-branded content, and only have a few people view your site each week.

These three types of digital media each have their advantages and disadvantages, which is why they shouldn't be used in isolation from each other.

Our goal is to determine where our clients are hanging out, and target our messaging at the right place and right time to get them interested in our products and services

Chapter 3: Finding the courage to look over your shoulder

No matter how far you go in life, no matter how successful you may become, no matter how happy you may seem to be; the time will come when in order to move to the next level within your life…you will face the challenge of having to look over your shoulder and assess the road you have traveled thus far.

Finding the courage to look over your shoulder, to face the many decisions you have made in this life can be a most daunting realization but is eventually something we all must do if we are to authentically deliver our message to the world. As nice as it would be, to only have favorable decisions to reflect upon when reviewing the footage of our past, it is as far from reality as the farthest planet is from earth.

Facing the past for me was for many years the single most terrifying aspect of living. I had buried so many memories; situations, abuses, and unanswered questions, that I felt these memories carried the weight of a million lifetimes of pain and regret. Due to my having been abused mentally, physically, sexually, and even spiritually during my childhood within the foster system, I found myself entering adulthood completely unprepared in how to even consider the digging out process.

When unpleasant situations find their way into a child's world, there seems to be an innate self-preservation system that automatically kicks in to keep the child as safe as possible, at least in my case there seemed to be. My second night within the foster care system was the final night of my innocence, for that was the night sexual abuser #1 introduced me to what true darkness really was. I remember clearly every detail of my abuser's deconstruction of what little remained of my already shattered childhood.

I remember everything from the smell of his spearmint chewing gum, to the way he switched his voice from dark and menacing to light and trusting, all with the ease of flipping a light switch. If I were able to physically remove each memory that I have from those dreadful years within the foster care system and place them atop one another, God only knows just how high the stack would reach.

The fact of the matter is, for the most part none of us can ever totally remove all the past from within the corners of our minds, but we can condition ourselves to look upon those memories with a renewed purpose. By understanding and then believing that nothing happens by accident, that everything has a purpose, we can begin the transfer of power back over to that side of ourselves that is designed to serve and impact our world in a positive way.

As children, we unwittingly accept everything that goes wrong within our lives and even sometimes within the lives of those close to us…as our fault. A child's innocence knows no other way than that of wanting everything to feel safe, to feel right, to love and to be loved in return. The mindset of a child however, does not last for very long, is oftentimes cut short by circumstances beyond the child's control. So how does one summon the courage to face the monsters that reside beneath the beds of our past? How exactly do we go about finding the courage to look over our shoulder and find meaning from all the past represents?

One of the methods I utilized in my journey of facing the past was to learn a new method of blame. For many years I found myself stuck, unable to truly move forward in my quest for true happiness and fulfillment, simply because I was wasting much of my energy blaming. I blamed my past for everything from being lonely to why I could not find happiness in any type of work I pursued. I spent so many years blaming the past, that before I realized it I had created an entirely new layer of bad memories, memories that when being completely honest I could only blame myself for.

The scales of justice finally began to turn in my favor when I authentically and consistently began the arduous task of forgiving. I first had to forgive myself for the things in my life that I had screwed up all on my own, and then I had to begin to forgive myself for blaming myself for all those things I had no control over from my childhood.

Once this process of forgiveness began in earnest, I was amazed by just how quickly so much within my life began to change for the better. Suddenly I was attracting more likeminded people into my space, others who just like me were on a journey of enlightenment, others who wanted nothing more than to get past whatever obstacles stood between them and their desire to share their message with the masses.

The art of forgiveness is by no means easy to master, however when layered with purpose and passion for something one feels they are not willing to live without, the process can deliver incredible results and bring forth healing beyond compare. When we begin to blast those demons from our past with the power of forgiveness, we make way for incredible growth opportunities and deep levels of personal development to take root.

For many years I experienced huge amounts of shame and remorse for carrying around what I had come to believe to be "baggage". I had always associated anyone with baggage as someone who was undesirable, someone who in most cases was more trouble than they were worth. I had fallen prey to the misconception that if I were someone who possessed a past that was anything other than perfect, that my chances of someday finding love, personal fulfillment, and overall joy were next to impossible.

Once I accepted and then embraced the mindset that it was okay for me to have happiness, something wonderful but also unexpected began to happen. Suddenly, those very things that I for most of my life had considered baggage, those undesirable badges of shame that had seemingly tattooed themselves into my spirit, they each began to take on new meaning…new purpose.

I then, as each of you will as well...began to realize that for me to embark upon that journey of a lifetime, to genuinely seek my destiny, I would need some baggage. No journey of considerable import can be taken without some baggage, if only a carry on...something is required to contain those items necessary for the journey. My problem with carrying baggage in the past was twofold; firstly, I was carrying too much unnecessary baggage, bags that for the most part did not even belong to me.

Secondly, I was over packing...dragging along many things that would be no use to me once I arrived at my destination in life.

In retrospect, I now understand just how important finding the courage to look over your shoulder is. The ability to confront whatever issues from the past that are preventing you from living the life you so desire and deserve, is not something that is achieved easily, but with courage, strength, and determination...it can be done.

More good news about what you can expect once you have confronted the past by looking over your shoulder, once you have cleared away even a portion of the rubble, you will begin to understand that beneath that very rubble is where you will find the core elements of your message to the masses.

Many believe that by allowing ourselves to become vulnerable, by sharing our complete stories, we are thereby shooting ourselves in the foot. We wear our histories like a ball and chain instead of the banner of courage and preservation it truly represents.

Once you have gathered your message from beneath those misguided regrets of the past, you will then be inclined to dust off your message and prepare it for delivery to those within the world that have been waiting for all it is that you have to say.

In conclusion, it is paramount that you fully understand all that this chapter is attempting to impart, if for any reason you feel now or even later in the book that you still have not completely been able to grasp the concepts contained herein, I encourage you to read and reread this chapter as often as you must in order to begin this vital process.

There are many elements of the past which are responsible for those hurdles that continually prevent us from reaching our fullest potential. The responsibility of removing these hurdles belongs to each of us, to allow anything that hinders your progression towards true joy and happiness falls under the jurisdiction of self-sabotage.

Nothing in life that is truly worthwhile is obtained easily, everything lasting must be built, must be worked for. Obtaining the honor of being able to share your message with the masses must be taken with the utmost seriousness. Once you have been granted the green light, once you begin experiencing the opening of doors that allow you access to the hearts and minds of others, the stakes in this life are greatly increased.

This is a serious on taking, this sharing of one's message...but it is also one of the most rewarding honors known to mankind. The ability to positively influence others, to take them by the hand and lead them through oftentimes dark and treacherous pathways can only be accomplished when your message is authentic and delivered in the manner which life delivered it to you…raw and uncut. Truth is the only thing within the universe that I believe never changes, so do whatever you must do to ensure that your message never becomes a "version".

True forgiveness of the past frees you up to once and for all view your message as it was intended from the moment your never-ending story began. Removing the clutter from your past can only aid you in your quest to help others to do the same.

As I mentioned at the beginning of this chapter, this will not be easy, it will be the one task that will make you want to give up, to quit…time and time again. This chapter contains the word "courage" within its' title, and that is for a good reason; it is courage that will stand with you when the baggage of the past attempts to convince you that you cannot live without it. It will be courage that will whisper to you to never forget that you have already forgiven those chains that once bound you to the past; therefore, you no longer need to fear their exposure.

It will be courage; your body guard for life, which will accompany you everywhere that destiny, shall lead. Never forget this as you embark upon what only a handful in this world can even dream of…and that is, impacting this world for good in the sharing of your message to the masses.

Chapter 4: Establishing Credibility, Expertise & Trust

Technology: an evil temptress for productivity…

Every successful relationship, whether it be business or personal, begins with the same foundation for success… the building of credibility, expertise, and trust. In business, the most effective form of advertising is always going to be "word of mouth", and that certainly holds true in the world of professional speaking!

Most of the books, webinars, and workshops out there will tell you that if you are effectively and consistently branding yourself properly, you can often times expect to receive at least one referral from any speaking gig, paid or unpaid. I personally believe that even if you do not receive a referral from a speaking gig immediately, all is not lost. From the moment you begin the process of searching for a speaking gig, your primary job is that of building credibility, expertise, and trust.

Let's think about this for a moment; imagine that Jane was an audience member at a speech you delivered recently on the current state of education in America and now she is at a dinner party, standing in a circle of her peers who are all sharing stories. Jane: "That's interesting Jim, I was actually at a conference just last week where the keynote speaker was saying the very same thing." Jim: "Really? What conference did you attend, and do you remember the keynote speaker's name? What was their keynote topic?"

Boom! Instantly, there is an open opportunity for Jane to become a member of your salesforce. If you have done your job as a professional speaker and have achieved the objective of those who hired you, Jane should easily be able to articulate the takeaway components of your speech, and hopefully remember your name as well. Imagine the countless opportunities one awesome speech after the next can afford you when you have 500-1,000 people like Jane out there sharing their excitement regarding you and your speaking abilities!

So, what do we need to do as speakers to ensure that we are consistently leaving not only our audience members in awe, but those meeting planners and decision makers who ultimately have the last word in who gets the gig or not? It's quite simple… we must effectively lay a valid foundation of credibility, expertise and trust!

Now, I wonder how many of you even noticed that in the final line of the preceding paragraph, I stated "a *VALID* foundation of credibility, expertise and trust." The reason I stress 'valid', is because when initially beginning one's journey into professional speaking, it can be tempting to add a bit of "fluff" to one's bio, credentials, or one sheet. Let's face it, how many times in the past when filling out a job application or preparing a resume, we added a few extra months on to the experience section, or perhaps exaggerated one element or another of our job description or achievements? Perhaps you have never fallen prey to what I am describing here, but trust me... many others have, and even if it worked in the past and you were never found out, it is simply NOT something you should even consider when building a brand/persona in professional speaking.

Each element of your speaker package must be clear, consistent, and honest. I remember that when I began to initially compile my speaker package so that I would have something to get out there, something to provide the decision makers with... it seemed I had very little to build on.

Eventually, I learned that a little of the truth goes a long way. It is always best to only deliver the facts when attempting to create those first impressions, although it may be tempting to embellish a bit here or there, presenting as honest a representation as possible works out best in the long run.

So where do we start, what do I say that can establish credibility, expertise and trust? Let's address each of these crucial elements individually, shall we?

Establishing Credibility

CREDIBILITY:
- "The quality of being trusted and believed in."
- "The quality of being convincing or believable."

In both versions of the definition of Credibility, you will notice one word that is consistent...QUALITY! The fact that *quality* is built into the very root of the definition of credibility, lets us know that being credible is not something that simply happens. It must be earned, it must be built, it must be organic.

Exemplifying credibility can be conveyed to decision makers and meeting planners in a variety of ways, but one method that stands out is the tried and true *TESTIMONIAL.*

A variety of short, but heartfelt testimonials within your website, online profile, social media sites, and speaker one sheet, within/on your book cover, or even somewhere within your speaker bio… is a powerful and effective way to allow others who know and have experienced you, speak to the credibility of your character as well as your work.

In most cases, an effective testimonial is anywhere between 3 to 5 lines. When researching this, you will find a variety of positions which speak to how many lines is preferred when citing a testimonial, we suggest you adapt to whichever format suits the needs of your overall message. Yet another format that works wonders in conveying credibility is the **video testimonial.**

A video testimonial achieves the same objective as the written testimonial, only in video format. A video testimonial is also quite powerful when establishing credibility as it allows the viewer to actually *live and experience* the level of excitement/trust that the reviewer has for you. Nothing works more quickly and effectively than hearing something "straight from the horse's mouth!"

Establishing Expertise

EXPERTISE: "Expert skill or knowledge in a particular field."

The element of expertise is the next vital component we need to begin working to establish that we are worthy of sharing our knowledge and message. Expertise in any area can be achieved in a variety of ways and is intended to prove without a doubt to decision makers and our audiences that we indeed know what we are talking about.

The most common forms of proving expertise are: certifications, advanced degrees, and licensees; but what if your expertise is founded on a non-traditional format?

Here are a few additional ways one can provide substantial insight into expertise: books and articles that you have published, awards you may have won, interviews and media attention you may have received, life experience and community involvement. In today's world, it is not uncommon for non-traditional students, those returning to college or university later in life, to receive "life experience" credits toward certain degrees they may be pursuing.

For example, a person who has owned and operated a career coaching business for several years could very easily receive "expert" status recognition from their peers simply due to their program having consistently been recognized for providing a level of service that far outshines the competition.

To be perceived as an expert in any area, one merely must have established a reputation for extraordinary knowledge and a proven track record of competency in the area(s) or field(s) in question.

In conclusion remember, **"Every expert was once a beginner."**

Establishing Trust

TRUST: "firm belief in the reliability, truth, ability, or strength of someone or something."

The element of trust is one that is never built on the "sprint" theory in as much as it is built on the "marathon" theory. Trust is, in most instances, the grout or glue if you will, that bonds all the other elements together. Most business and personal relationships alike; they have a lengthy track record of success and can trace that successful record back to having built a solid foundation for that relationship based on trust.

We commonly hear trust referred to as something that must be built or earned, and that is exactly how the process works. The trust element is incorporated into the plan with each and every move you make.

Let's consider how the element of trust plays into something as simple or basic as a professional head shot. When seeking out the professional services for a marketable business head shot, there are many elements that contribute to the conveying of what the overall objective of the headshot is… the building of trust.

Many publicists, professional stylists, and marketing guru's will go to great lengths to ensure that their client has not only the proper setting for the head shot, but specific lighting and theme as well. Should the client be full body or simply head and shoulders? What colors work best with the client's skin tone, hair color, eye color? What colors speak to the market that the client is aiming for? Should the client smile or be more serious? These questions, ideas, and considerations are all vital to the overall success of the professional head shot for one reason… the conveyance of TRUST.

Whether your professional head shot is going to be used on your one sheet, book cover (front/back or inside), your banner, business card, social media profile pic, or in/on a brochure for your next speaking gig or conference, it must be multi-faceted; *it must* get you noticed, and *it must* convince the viewer that you can be trusted.

Recap

To recap: The foundation for all that you are building within your professional speaking career, business career, or personal life should always be built with these elements in mind:

- Establishing Credibility
- Establishing Expertise
- Establishing Trust

With these elements firmly planted within your process, you are certain to build a following that will remain loyal, steadfast, and supportive of not only what you do within your life/business today, but through all the great things you will accomplish in the years ahead as well.

For those who are negligent in this area of the process, it is almost impossible to go back and begin again once the structure begins to crumble, and without these elements… crumble it will. So be patient, remember that this is a marathon and not a sprint. Be honest, purposeful, and consistent in all that you do when growing your message to the masses, and your foundation built on credibility, expertise, and trust will never fail you, it will never let you down!

Words to remember: "Once the cement is dry, you can't go back!"

Chapter 5: Truth or Consequences

Do you solemnly swear to tell the truth, the whole truth, and nothing but the truth...so help you God?

That is the statement that for hundreds of years a person who was about to testify in a court of law had to agree to, whether they followed through on this promise or not. So why do you think it is so important that the truth be agreed to be told when testifying in a court of law? Furthermore, why do you think for hundreds of years people were made to not only swear, but place their hand on a Bible, and complete the entire process with; "so help me God".

Obviously, this was primarily due to the fact that the forefathers of The United States Of America believed that as a primarily Christian society, this would forevermore be a means of intimidating anyone who should even consider bending the truth or outright lying. This oath was Americas method of forcing all those who held someone else's fate in their hands with the story they told, into doing what was expected of any morally sound American; tell the truth.

The portion of this brief but poignant history lesson that I personally feel holds the most merit, is that the swearing in oath was primarily designed to remind the many "story tellers" that made their way in and out of

America's courtrooms of the seriousness of their moment in the spotlight.

Although the spotlight of a speaker or influencer may seem very different than that of the one which glares upon a witness in a courtroom, it truly is not so different at all. In fact, a speaker must be held to an even higher level of accountability than the witness is. A witness in a courtroom after all, has but the life of one or a few at most within their powerful grasp, whereas a speaker may have influence over the lives of thousands at a time. A witness in most cases is only a witness once or a handful of times at most over a lifetime, whereas a speaker has influence over thousands, perhaps millions of people countless times over the span of a successful speaking career.

Each of us in planning what our speaking career will look like, in that careful creation of the blueprint of a lifetime, will invest thousands of hours meticulously considering each element. But no element of this masterpiece is or ever will be more important, more crucial to the development and continued success of your dream of speaking…than the power which is contained within the truth.

The truth as far as I know, is the only creation within the universe that NEVER changes. The importance of truth is sprinkled in most everything throughout history that is of any import, and that has lasted the test of time. If you were to ask most people to quote one line from Shakespeare, the majority of those asked would respond; "To thine own self be true". The truth is powerful for many reasons, but again I personally believe that the greatest benefit of the truth, is that it never changes.

So why an entire chapter speaking to the importance of truth, the answer to that question is answered within this chapter's title: CONSEQUENCES!

In March of 1940 when the producers of the radio show "Truth or Consequences", hosted by Ralph Edwards chose the show's title, I doubt very seriously that they even tossed around the idea of calling the show "Truth and Consequences". It is obvious to me exactly why the show was titled as it was, for when there is truth which always stands alone…in all ways that matter, there are no true consequences.

Now some might say; how can that be when innocent people are wrongly convicted all the time? This example is exactly why we should see the power which the truth is. Whenever a wrongly convicted person is proven to be innocent, is it not the truth that set them free, that exonerated them? Is it then not the falsehood or untruth that is ultimately exposed? I get it, the many horrors which the wrongly convicted person was forced to endure in no shape or form seems fair or right, but we must remember that no matter what…this was nonetheless a scene within this persons never ending story.

So how does this tie in to the building of my speaking career you might be asking yourself? Well, let's consider how broadly it is accepted today when building out one's resume to "fluff it up a bit". If a person only worked at company "A" for 4 years and 9 months, most people would think nothing at all of simply "rounding up" to reflect 5 years of employment at company "A". Although this may seem minuscule in the broad scheme of things, it nonetheless holds within it the power to cause the person seeking employment to lose a opportunity if the truth is ever revealed.

Just as this worst-case scenario referenced above could very easily become a reality, so can the very same thing become a reality to the speaker who feels the need to "fluff up" their unique message to the masses.

In my over 24 years of event planning, I always planned every event from what I termed a best-case scenario to the worst-case scenario. This process never failed in providing me multiple options to consider in making each decision I was forced to make along the way. When considering which road is the best road, it is always a decision made based on sound judgement when that decision is rooted in what one knows to be true.

Many of life's most crucial decisions, those decisions that in retrospect prove to have been life altering, are in most cases decisions based on instinct, that gut feeling we all possess. How many times have you heard or even said; "Wow, so and so really has great instincts"? Well how do you think that person developed those "great instincts", was it by chance or were they developed?

I personally believe we all have the capability to condition whether we possess great instincts or not. By consistently striving to be as genuine, as authentic as possible in all things, we are conditioning ourselves to be lifetime subscribers to truth and all that truth represents.

A huge part of first finding one's true voice, is finding that message within you that has the power to change and influence the masses in a positive way. It is the ability to not question what you know to be true, those things that innately feel, sound, or simply resonate as right.

There is but one road which leads to this moment, this moment of truth, and that road is paved with consistency, determination, and passion. It is imperative to implement the ground rules for exactly how you intend to play the game and be committed to play it in this manner for life.

Our messages as speakers must always be the completeness which is only found in truth, there can be no versions, no little white lies, no bending of the truth. Life has given each one of us a story, a message that is worth telling, but that story must be presented in its fullness, not in whatever version feels safe at any given moment.

Remember, one of the greatest benefits of the truth is that one never has to remember what they said, if the truth is spoken today…it will still be the same exact truth millions of years from now.

By remaining true and authentic in all that you do, there is never any fear of exposure for something not quite being the truth. By remaining true and authentic in all that you do, you can embrace the universal gift that can only be received when one allows the magic to pour through you and not be reliant upon trying to force it from you.

If your message should one day reach the masses as I believe it shall, do not drag anything with you to that jubilation day that has even 1% chance of destroying all that you have worked so hard to achieve.

Face whatever needs to be faced, forgive whatever needs to be forgiven, and release whatever needs to be released. Once you have accomplished this, your truth, your voice, your message will have no choice but to soar to levels you could have never reached without life's shadow beside you. I encourage you to walk bravely into the shadow of truth, for it will never betray or abandon you, for when walking in truth there are never any consequences…only blessings.

Why Would Anyone Want to Listen to Me?

Each of us has our own unique belief systems, our own unique ground zero, and this is the runway wherein your journey must begin. To have adequate room in which to take off, one must have something far greater than ones' self to believe in when taking off.

When I first began to consider the then "ludicrous" idea of my one day sharing my story with the masses, I could see no reason whatsoever why anyone would ever be interested in hearing anything I might have to say.

Today, I speak in a variety of arenas to a variety of audiences, and presently find it near impossible to consider not doing what I so very much love to do. So how did I go from thinking my dream of public speaking was something far outside my wheelhouse, to living my dream...full time? It was by no means easy, but then it obviously was not impossible either.

The beginning of believing in this dream for me was my deeply rooted desire (and need) for inner-healing. I was nearing my mid-fifties, running out of entrepreneurial test runs to pursue, and beginning to feel the true pull of urgency which was screaming to my spirit that I had better get started or I most likely would never experience my true destiny.

I now realize that most of the time I spent in my life doing everything but sharing my story with others, was both a combination of "learning my way to the starting line", fear of the unknown, and good old fashion procrastination.

I also now realize that each one of those days leading up to my starting line were necessary, were mandatory in the creation of my never-ending story. Not one of those days was wasted, not one moment of my "on the job training" was by accident, and not one lesson learned was essential than the next.

I know it to be true that my reality of today is happening today, because it was timed and destined for…today.

Because I know that right about now you are beginning to become a bit antsy, wondering what the big answer is to the big question that began this chapter; "Why would anyone want to listen to me?", let me get right to it.

The reason anyone would want to listen to anything you might have to share is simple, it's because your story is and always will be…greater than you! Each of us takes for granted (in most cases) the enormous impact that our stories potentially have on the world around us. Not initially understanding this vital concept is something I personally believe each person who has ever struggled and scratched their way towards destiny has had to deal with.

Many of you most likely believe that my personal story of having endured horrible situations throughout my 5 years within the foster system is what has brought my story to the stage, but that could not be further from the truth. It is more about the stories of others I have encountered along the way which have consistently fed my need for healing and inspired me to continue no matter what.

If I had relied solely upon the story I was living at any given time in my life, I would have most assuredly missed out on the true moments of change and growth that had afforded me by the courageous survivors I met along the way. It was due to those who were able to summon the power of their personal truths and then share those truths with me, that I was able to begin the healing process which has led me to my own truths.

Our experiences and all that comes with them are lessons, those lessons if learned; are then transformed into stories, and those stories then have the potential to become messages. The reason I believe that so many are never able to find their message for the masses, is because they have never acknowledged the mandatory requirement that insists that before we can take on the responsibility of sharing anything to the masses, we first must understand the why of the lessons we experience in life.

Here's what I mean by that, let's say I am a person who consistently blames everything that does not feel good in my life on someone or something else?

If I am never able to at least consider how I may have done something better, how my contribution could have been different to the overall outcome; then most likely I will never get the full benefit of the experience and therefore miss the true lesson contained within the experience.

I find it interesting how whenever I need to remove myself from a world of depression, doubt, or fear…, I need only do something positive for someone or some situation outside of myself. However, whenever I find myself inserting "I" or "me" into the equation of any problem-solving technique, I focus more internally, and the situation becomes worse and quickly can take on a direction of self-sabotage. So again, (personally speaking) I believe that many of us miss our opportunities to share our messages on a large scale, primarily since we are not doing the work necessary on a small scale.

Discovering the truth which lives within each story we experience, can only be achieved by seeking the truth within each lesson we endure. This is the process which then allows us the same opportunity to share our messages on a larger as when we were learning and living this very message on a smaller scale.

In conclusion, I would be remiss in my obligation to allow my truths to find you because of coming through me and not from me, if I did not remind you of the most important element of all in successfully growing your message to the masses.

 Please, if you only remember one thing from this entire book, please remember this; there can be only one road to sharing your message to the masses, and that road must be paved in truth. You must be willing to commit to not only the good times that will indeed be yours once you begin sharing your incredible message with the world, but to the countless moments along the way when your truths will certainly make you feel as if you are unwelcomed, misunderstood, and very much unloved.

There will be many challenges in remaining loyal to the truth of your message, but it is the only way to assure that you will one day deliver your message to the masses exactly as The Creator has intended; intact and unchanged.

For each lesson that you have learned in life, for every hardship that you have endured, for every tear you have shed…there is a reason. You have already lived the hard part, so face that truth and begin embracing your destiny, begin the separating of truth from fiction, remove fear and replace it with faith.

This life provides countless "opportunity intersections", and as you approach each, be encouraged and know that whomever or whatever is making its' way towards you has been looking forward to receiving what you have for them, just as much as you have been looking forward to sharing it.

So, there it is, the answer to the question that attempts to discourage, redirect, and rob; "Why would anyone want to listen to me?" Because…YOU have a message that MUST be shared, a story that MUST be told…that's why!

Chapter 6: Your Never-Ending Story

In the 1984 movie The Never-Ending Story, the message delivered was poignant and very much to the point; without our dreams, without imagination, without heart, without caring for others...humanity basically doesn't have a reason to exist, we would be "nothing".

In the constant quest to unearth our unique message to the world, a quest that so many of us find to be challenging, many of the answers sought can be found residing within our own never-ending stories.

I was just today sharing with someone on a coaching call, the fact that I believe my own never-ending story was already being written long before I entered this world. My birth mother, I am sure began considering what would eventually be a life-changing decision for both herself and me...long before she delivered me on July 4th, 1962. Upon deciding that she would give me up for adoption, my birth mother could never have known that the woman she would entrust my upbringing to, would die prematurely; thereby catapulting me into the arms of the state foster care system only 9 years later.

So, as you see...my never-ending story was indeed already being decided, already being written for me in many aspects, long before I played any actual role in the writing of it. My purpose in siting my own life as an example... is merely meant to bring light to the fact that although we each are the primary author of our individual never ending stories, there are nonetheless those decisions made by others which contribute greatly to the storylines of our lives.

The idea that outside forces contribute much to the initial shaping of our never-ending stories is where I believe many of us lose our way. For many years I blamed those decisions made on my behalf by others, decisions that set certain paths in motion, decisions that I personally never had any control over whatsoever, for just about everything that did not work within my life.

As a child, was it wrong that I blamed my adopted mother for suddenly dying and leaving me to fend for myself within a system that was designed to stunt my ability to dream? Was it wrong for me to blame my birth mother for not sticking it out, for abandoning me, for me believing this is what truly happened until I met her at age 32?

Was it wrong that I blamed the 7 sexual abusers I endured while living within the system for robbing me of what little childhood innocence remained, only after my spirit had already been raped by death?

Was it wrong that I blamed not understanding that it was okay to be gay on the weight of the many other scarlet letters and badges of shame I was forced to wear due to my status of foster kid?

Was it wrong that I blamed my inability to love and to be loved in return on the countless hollow eyes I was forced to stare into over the years, eyes of the adults who were given the charge to protect me, to keep me safe?

The answer to each of these questions is a resounding no! As a child I had no other choice but to bury my feelings deep within the soothing comfort found only in the placing of blame. As I began to leave the protective shell of childhood however; I began to realize that this solace I had become so very comfortable with, this blanket of blame I had embroidered with so many casualties…was beginning to feel like more of a burden than a comfort.

So, what was the cause of this slow yet sudden transformation?

Forgiveness! I was beginning to understand the power of healing that comes only through time, and with that healing came the art of forgiveness. I found that as the past began to move further and further away, so too did the painful memories.

I in no way mean to say that the pain was completely washed away…gone, but the sting of loss began to fade and, in its place, small seeds of hope began to grow in the form of dreams.

Because of the sobering manner in which my childhood was forced to come to an abrupt halt, places within my mind which previously sheltered ideals of Santa Claus and The Easter Bunny, now became the mantle place for my dreams.

The most wonderful aspect of realizing the power in writing your own never-ending story, is that you are introduced or reintroduced in many cases to things you once felt had left your world forever…but have been within you all along, simply waiting for the perfect time to reveal themselves to you.

Most of us have at least some memories that we wish we could forget, some situations that we would rather have never been a part of, and at least a few regrets that truly belong to someone or something else. Life could not be life if it did not have the ups and downs that serve as proof of life.

Many people miss the mark in life because they are constantly seeking that life when everything will be perfect, when all will at long last be completely smooth. I often remind myself that a life of smooth is the last thing I should be hoping for, a life-line that is smooth is no life-line at all, it is however a flat-line…that universal sign that life is no longer present.

It is in the ups and downs that we will always find life, where we will always locate that pulse which is the universal sign that life is present.

A never-ending story is legacy, a never-ending story is history, a never-ending story is imprint, and we each have one within ourselves but unearthing it can be a challenge. If one remembers to consistently seek the good which eventually can be found in every experience, in every lesson that life gives, then and only then will the magic of the never-ending story be unlocked.

To share your message with the masses you must be willing to bear the cost of possessing the honor. To influence others daily, you must first be influenced by others and this exchange will take on many shapes and forms before your never-ending story is written in its entirety.

A never-ending story is proof that you have done the work required to dig from beneath whatever falsehoods, whatever lies, whatever circumstances have continually worked to remove any desire from you to even care about your never-ending story. A never-ending story is what will continue long after you have transitioned from this world into whatever is next for you. A never-ending story lives on and on…it continues to provide that much needed pulse to the circle of life. So, face your past, forgive in the present, and then embark upon your future…for it is there that your never-ending story will continue to live forever.

The truth you share today will be the same truth that someone 500 or 5000 years from now will share, and how do I know that? It's simple...TRUTH, it's the only thing within the universe that NEVER changes! You have already lived the hard part, so take those truths with you for you have earned them by simply living life, your very own never-ending story!

Chapter 7: Opportunity Intersections

Have you ever considered just how important intersections are within our lives? I have, and the thing I think I love most about intersections is that it brings travelers from all directions to one common place of crossing.

Just as the intersections we each walk, bike, or drive towards in life are filled with things we have no way of predicting will arrive at the exact time we do…the same is true of the intersections we encounter in life, *opportunity intersections*.

When moving towards an intersection of any type, it is not simply about those things we have no way of knowing, it is also about those things we do know. For example, when approaching any intersection, we know that we will either be forced to stop, slow down (yield), or be allowed to shoot directly through. Again, the same is true of each opportunity intersection we encounter in life.

While there are few constants, few things that we know without question will come into play at each intersection, there is fact that will never change and that is; no matter how good our instincts or vision…we will never be able to see around the corners of those intersections we are approaching. Just as humans we do not possess the ability to bend our vision around a corner, neither can we bend our ability to access or ascertain what is around the corners of each opportunity intersection we find ourselves approaching in life.

Many of us forget that intersections are vital components in every journey. Intersections allow for a balanced flow of traffic from all directions, intersections provide a sense of politeness wherein each traveler must wait their turn to proceed through the intersection.

How many times have you found yourself as you approach that intersection where the light is yellow and has been for a while, quickly deciding if you should risk blowing through or should you simply hit the brakes and stop?

Each time I find myself in this position, the very first thing I do whether I blow through or make a somewhat abrupt stop…is look in my rearview mirror or at the surrounding participants to see who all has observed my last second decision.

Why do you suppose I do this, look around? Is it to see if others are sizing up my level of responsibility as a fellow traveler? Is it because perhaps just a small portion of me is feeling guilty for not being prepared for stopping? Who knows, perhaps it is a little bit of everything, but no matter what the reason is I always am left feeling that somehow, I could have made a safer decision and then I ask myself…why didn't I? This example is not unlike what we each do within our lives when approaching life's intersections, those intersections of opportunity.

The primary purpose of intersections in the first place is to ensure the safety of any and everyone who must cross an intersection, the rules are in place because it is not uncommon for those traveling in all directions to become distracted, be in a hurry, or any number of situations that could very well prove fatal if some sense of order is not established.

Statistics prove that 40% of all crashes involve intersections, the second largest category of accidents. 50% of crashes at intersections are of a *serious* nature and some 20% of *fatal* crashes occur there.

So now that we see how important traffic intersections truly are in our world, let's look at why the intersections of opportunity within our lives are equally important if not more so.

Something we have touched on from time-to-time throughout this book so far, is the utter importance of facing the past in all its fullness, and the manner in which we approach opportunity intersections warrants this reflection as well.

When speeding through life, many times we miss opportunity intersections in life. We are exceeding the speed limit, in a mad rush either running to or from something. Speed limits are set for reasons in life, and often we make the conscience decisions to ignore the posted warning signs. The limits to what we can do…safely, are placed within our journey for our own good and must be adhered to if we truly wish to reach our destination in one piece.

The primary way in which opportunity intersections differ from real life traffic intersections is found in the *interaction*. Opportunity intersections are a purposeful meeting that whatever you believe to be greater than yourself has set in motion long before you ever began your journey.

By reminding yourself each time you begin a new journey to be mindful of the opportunity intersections you will most assuredly encounter along the way, you create a much greater chance of fully benefiting from those intersections. By reminding yourself that your *destination* is in sync with your *destiny*, you are creating the very element which transforms "chance encounters" into opportunity.

Once you have completed the pre-journey check list; reminding yourself to remain calm along the way no matter what conditions you encounter, agreeing within yourself to keep your eyes on the intended path, and believing in your internal GPS system to get you to your destination safely, you can peacefully make your way towards the many intersections of opportunity that await along your route.

For those who become so overwhelmed with life that they neglect to complete the pre-journey checklist, they can in most cases be certain that they will encounter a plethora of unnecessary traffic jams, detours, and speeding tickets.

This journey called life has assigned a unique message for each of us who are courageous enough to get behind the wheel and remain there. Our messages will be shared with friends and family who are invited to ride along from time-to-time. Our messages will be shared with the occasional stranger that we offer a ride to, simply because they were stranded and needed roadside assistance. Our messages will even be shared with the sometimes-scary hitchhiker that we pull over for, even when something tells us this may not be such a good idea. You must never forget; each *intersection* is there to encourage *interaction,* and each *destination* is very much in sync with your *destiny.*

By consistently reminding yourself of these truths, you are immensely growing not only your opportunities to enjoy all the beauty along the journey, but you are increasing your opportunities to grow and share your message, to fulfill your calling in this world. Understanding and respecting each step of the journey, appreciating the sights along the way, slowing to a complete stop at each intersection, well…you get it, or at least I pray you will before finishing this book.

My deepest desire for each of you who is reading this, is that you each live a journey that is ticket free, stress free, doubt free, and most importantly…accident free. Take your time, plan for your journey by each day becoming a better version of yourself, and trust that your vehicle is road worthy. Do these things consistently and there is no doubt in my mind that you will change the lives of all you encounter along the way.

Opportunity intersections; those four ways stops in life that allow us to respect, acknowledge, take a deep breath, and continue on our way…may you have many as you grow your message for the masses, and beyond.

Developing a Sure-Fire Follow-Up System

This is where most people drop the ball!

Right the first time…

When I was a kid and would rush through any task or chore that forced my mom to call me back for a "re-do", I would hear this each and every time; *"If you don't seem to have time to do it properly the first time, how is it you always seem to be able to find the time to do it over?"*

Okay, if I am to be completely honest, I must admit that maintaining my follow-up system is the area that I struggle the most in. Yes, I admit it, but I must also admit that when I am on top of my follow-up game, my level of the successful close is greatly increased! I personally believe (at least in my own case), that one of the reasons that follow-up is such an issue, is that follow-up on the exterior is nowhere near as exciting as when the chase for the gig initially begins.

So, what is follow-up exactly?

Follow-up is, "a continuation or repetition of something that has already been started or done…"

Developing a sure-fire follow-up system is crucial for several reasons:

- Provides a checks/balances system for all your efforts

- Keeps the door of communication open with future potential clients
- Allows a reference point for ascertaining what is working or not with your marketing
- Increases the opportunity to capitalize on ALL your efforts
- Teaches you how to "read between the lines", i.e. learning what the client is and is not telling you
- Prevents opportunities from slipping through the cracks

A Checks/Balances System

Being honest about your efforts

There are countless ways in which to establish a sound and effective follow-up system, but whichever type you should implement, it should fit nicely within your lifestyle and personality type.

Here's what I mean by that; let's say you are more of a "visually stimulated" person. You most likely will do best by implementing a system which allows you to see your follow-up needs, for instance a wall chart or dry erase board. Personally, this is how I do it; I maintain a dry erase calendar. I have it in a prominent place within my office directly behind my desk so that whenever seated at my desk, I have no choice, but to see what follow-up needs my attention.

I found that by implementing a resource that in effect "saved me from myself", I was able to achieve far greater results and benefits from all of my efforts. Before my wall calendar, I simply *attempted* to keep track of which bids were still pending within a notebook. Although the notebook worked nicely for logging my follow-up needs, I soon found that I still was not getting much follow-up work accomplished due to the fact that I was slowly, but surely burying my follow-up notebook beneath files, paper work, or anything else that assisted in my need for the "out of sight, out of mind" form of self-sabotage.

If you find that you are more of a "techy" type, perhaps your follow-up system would work best if maintained within a device of your choice. There is a plethora of apps available to assist in the organization of data, so if you are tech savvy, I highly recommend you find the app that best suits your follow-up needs and not simply download it but utilize it to the fullest.

When initially starting out in professional speaking, of course most of us do not have the benefit of using a speaker agent or agency to seek out those speaking gigs we so desperately desire. In most cases, we must do all of the work ourselves. Most of us when just getting started in our speaking careers are still forced to maintain our day job, which means that basically we are constantly attempting to fit our speaking career needs in wherever we can find a spare hour or two. Does it not make sense then to capitalize on all of the hard work we put into the launching of our life's journey... the sharing of our message with the masses? Of course, it does!

So, let's continue the process of developing a sure-fire follow-up system and remember... each element is designed to remind us of the importance of being honest with ourselves regarding being as thorough as possible from the beginning of the gig search, all the way to the payoff of getting hired!

Keeping the Door of Communication Open

Each time I submit my speaker package for consideration, I cannot help but feel an elevated sense of excitement when hitting the send button or dropping my speaker kit within the mail. Each time I throw my hat into the ring of opportunity, I truly believe that this speaking opportunity is meant for me. But as can oftentimes happens, a day or two later, I begin the "worry section" of the getting hired process. It is not only common, but quite normal to begin being concerned about the following:

1. I wonder if they've looked at my submission yet, and if so, what are they thinking?
2. Did I do everything within my power to accurately represent myself and my message?
3. I wonder what the competition submitted, is my work as good as theirs? These are just a few examples of the many questions we begin to ponder almost immediately upon submitting ourselves for a potential speaking gig. Like I mentioned, this is a normal part of the process, but is also the opportunity for you to channel this energy into something positive and that is

accomplished by directing your attention to your follow-up system.

The moment you have submitted your work, you should place that potential opportunity into your follow-up system. Along the way, you will develop your own personal style of how you follow-up with potential clients; the follow-up email seeking acknowledgement of receipt of your submission, how you respond to that acknowledgement and how you open the door to the next communication. Don't expect that you will be able to use the exact same technique each time. Since each of the decision makers you encounter will each have their own personal style, it is up to you to pick up on that style and utilize it to your benefit during the hiring process.

By incorporating anything that the decision maker shares with you along the way that you later may utilize within your communication, you could very well be creating that defining moment wherein the decision maker sees that you were indeed listening. That alone could be the very thing that separates you from the rest of the crowd and gets you HIRED!

Keep track of anything that the client shares of a personal nature. Take copious notes and keep your fingers on the pulse of the decision-making process based on what your client is sharing with you. If the client says that the decision is now in the hands of a committee or some other rung of the organizational hierarchy, it is crucial that you learn how to extract a sense for when that portion of the decision making is expected to transpire, thereby providing you with a timeline for your next communication within your follow-up procedure.

In my experience, the decision maker simply gets buried in the many other tasks that they are accountable for within their job description. This is what I refer to as "falling asleep at the wheel". Often, if I have heard nothing from the client regarding how things are going based on the most recent information provided me, I will give the situation a fair amount of time (a couple days), and then I will reach out to the client, give them a brief nudge, and then await the client's response. If I do not receive any response to my nudge, I then make note of that and move to my next follow-up technique accordingly.

Never underestimate how many potential gigs have been lost simply due to the decision maker "falling asleep at the wheel". By developing a portion of your follow-up system that provides a non-threatening "brief nudge", you just might be surprised at how many jobs you can snatch from the clutches of your competition, simply because you had a process in place that kept you awake to the possibilities.

Remember, anything is possible if the door to communication is open.

What's working vs. what's not

Another beneficial aspect of maintaining a stellar follow-up system is that it provides you the data needed to assess what is working within your bidding process and what is not. By taking extra care in documentation (especially in the early stages), you are providing yourself with the means to cross reference what exactly you did that either led you to the hire or did not.

When successful in procuring the speaking gig, which you are certain to do, your follow-up must continue, and vigorously. The post-hire follow-up is where you can obtain some of the most crucial information that will aid in your creating that sure-fire follow-up system you so desire. Once you have been hired, you should further separate yourself from your competition by eliciting as much feedback from your client as you possibly can during the entire process. This is from the moment you receive notification of the hire through the review/testimonial, which you should ask for the day after your presentation.

The post-hire follow-up is where you can not only receive valuable insight/feedback from your client about how things proceeded from day one pertaining to your bidding procedure, but you can now find out much regarding your competition. I have personally saved myself many missteps simply by finding out from client's what things my competition did or did not do that resulted in my getting the gig. These insights are invaluable, and trust me, not many of your competitors will even consider doing this as a part of their follow-up system. Once again, you have further distanced yourself from the rest of the competition!

Reading Between the Lines

Right about now I am sure you are wondering, "what exactly does reading between the lines mean?" Reading between the lines is the technique you must adapt wherein you are training yourself to not proceed at any point of the bidding process, simply based on the information the potential client has provided. This is important especially when working within the many online speaker platforms that are available for us to procure speaking engagements.

Let's address how this pertains to online speaker platforms first. Most speaker platforms provide a template format for the client to use in building their speaking needs request. The client may not (which is usually the case) be tech savvy, which means they most likely will depend on the template format for providing the crucial information that you will use in making the decision whether this opportunity falls within your wheelhouse or not.

Many times, the budget can be anything other than what the client "actually" is working with, and the projected audience size can oftentimes be a "guesstimate". This would still affect not only your speaker fee, but in most cases, the amount the speaker site is charging you to bid on this opportunity. Therefore, you must carefully assess the budget regarding how it corresponds with the projected audience numbers. Do they match up?

Distance also plays a factor, if you quickly submit a bid on a gig without first considering the distance, what time is the gig, and what if it is early morning and 300 miles away? All these factors could cost you more than you bid on the gig, a horrible fact to be made aware of after you have won the speaking opportunity. I know this because it happened to me.

One more thing that I must warn you about when utilizing speaker sites:

- IF THE CLIENT DOES NOT HAVE A THEME FOR THE PRESENTATION, DO NOT BID!

When I first began using online speaker sites, it never dawned on me that nearly half of the jobs I found myself bidding on, the client had no idea of what their theme was! These bids were the equivalent to taring money up and throwing it in the air. Think about it: if the client does not know what the message they need to have conveyed to their audience, then how can they even begin seeking the perfect speaker to deliver that message?

These are a few examples of how important it is to not simply get caught up in the excitement of the bidding process with online speaker sites. Be patient and take your time to not only read what is contained within the request but look for that pertinent information which might be missing as well. Just as the saying goes, "It is not always about what someone says, as much as it is about what they leave out."

Take your time and read between the lines. It will not only save you money and valuable time, but it will prevent you from unnecessary perceived defeats as well.

Sealing the Cracks – Quit Losing Opportunities

Hopefully at this point, we have been successful in convincing you of just how very important a sure-fire follow-up system is, and the importance of having one implemented within your speaking business infrastructure.

With juggling, all that we must manage within our busy lives, it is crucial that we do not add to the already staggering amounts of confusion, disappointment, and feelings of defeat by allowing much of our hard work and dedication to fall through the cracks due to no follow-up system being in place.

Always approach your journey with best and worst-case scenarios, work your plan, your systems from front-to-back, and then from back-to-front. For those who are serious about reaching their goals of delivering their messages to the masses, implementation of a sound follow-up system will be a key component that will most certainly assist substantially in providing you a place at the table, an opportunity to share your message with the masses!

Chapter 8: Dropping the Bread Crumbs

How to Lead Decision Makers to Your Doorstep & Get Booked!

The goal in whether you are speaking your way to more business or speaking as a business, is to get paid for your message. Getting meeting planners and decision makers to question not if you are worth the money you are asking to share your story is no easy accomplishment.

The intricate process of leading decision makers to your doorstep is a process that requires as much dedication and energy (perhaps even more so), as the defining of one's message. Don't get me wrong, creating a clear and powerful message is paramount. However; if you do not have a proven system wherein you are able to convince the powers that hire that you are the obvious choice for their needs, your message will never reach it's intended mark, your audience.

To authentically represent yourself in the best light possible, you must introduce the required elements within your relationship with the decision maker from the word GO! Whether you are reaching out via email, text message, cover letter, speaker one sheet, speaker bio, or simply a phone call…never forget; "We only get one opportunity to make a first impression". Make it a positive and memorable one!

In our chapter "Establishing Credibility, Expertise, and Trust", we shared with you some proven techniques for successfully building the foundation in your relationship building with meeting planners and decision makers, now it's time to share with you exactly how to fold these ingredients into the overall recipe for becoming successfully hired.

Just as it was within the children's story Hansel and Gretel, where the children purposefully dropped bread crumbs meant to provide a means for them to find their way should they get lost. The same theory applies here. Our system of dropping bread crumbs, is meant not only to provide a pathway of intrigue that leads the meeting planner/decision maker to your doorstep, but also to provide you with a clear-cut system in which to always gain optimum leverage from all your efforts during the process of getting hired.

The breadcrumb dropping process is basically designed exactly like any essay you were called upon to write while in school. Each format should contain an *introduction*, a *body*, and a *conclusion*. There are additional requirements however that we shall discuss now, so let's begin with The Introduction.

The Introduction

As mentioned earlier, it matters not which avenue of communication you are utilizing to get yourself noticed by the meeting planner or decision maker. You will only be able to successfully draw them deeper into your message, your lair so-to-speak, by creating an authentic desire for them to want to know you better and begin to convince them of your likeability. As a reminder, know that you must never forget that you only have one opportunity to make a good first impression. Therefore, one must remain mindful at each step of the process to the importance of not forgetting what the objective is here – to get yourself hired!

Immediately after your salutation, the very first thing you should begin to establish is what you do and how it is that you do this thing differently than anyone else.

Example introduction verbiage & its elements

"Hi there, my name is Jane Marie Doe. I am a motivational speaker who strives to introduce each person I encounter to my systematic approach of discovering the tools required for living a more fulfilling life. I open new doors of possibility through the incorporation of *sound therapy, visual relaxation* techniques, and believe it or not, *olfactory sensory techniques*. My proven system of incorporating all of the senses has allowed me to help others find their way to a more productive life through sight, sound, and smell."

What Jane Marie Doe has effectively done has introduced herself by getting directly to what she feels is her **PURPOSE**: *"…strives to introduce each person I encounter…tools required for living a more fulfilling life."* The decision maker immediately has a bit of information that speaks to who Jane Marie Doe is even when she is not speaking before audiences.

This is accomplished when Jane states *"each person I encounter";* this plants a picture that Jane is vested in and believes so strongly in her purpose that she has incorporated her mission into her everyday life and not just when she is getting paid to share those beliefs.

The next example of breadcrumb dropping is when Jane says, *"I open new doors…possibilities".* In using the term "open new doors" as well as "possibilities", Jane creates an air of intrigue. It allows the decision maker to begin asking questions, and it begins the building of excitement by adding an element of curiosity into the introduction; and therefore, pulls the decision maker farther down the intended path.

The final element of Jane's introduction was yet another visual stimulant for the decision maker to consider. When Jane uses the term "incorporate" (which she uses twice), Jane again leads the decision maker further down the intended path by stating this in a way that makes the decision maker think "I wonder how she does that?"

Upon reading Jane's introduction, provided she has presented her message to the correct market and the ideal client, she most likely has achieved the desired effect of the introduction. The decision maker has an idea of the person Jane truly is, a few reasons to authentically "like" her, and some questions she will most likely want answered and will be prompted to continue her inquisition into whether Jane is the speaker she/he is looking to hire.

The Body

The body is where you begin to distance yourself from the pack of competitors who are vying for the same speaking gig you are. This is where you must use everything within your power to convince the decision maker that you know more about the subject they are looking for than anyone else, anywhere!

In the establishing of what makes you the best choice for hire, the way to optimally cover all the bases is to consistently attempt to think outside of the box. Thinking outside of the box basically allows you the freedom to utilize the value of all your accomplishments; those that fall within the parameters of traditional credentials as well as the non-traditional.

If a person has been a member of an advocacy group, volunteer organization, civic organization, or any membership organization which the involvement therein speaks directly to their voice as an authority, then these involvements most assuredly can be included when establishing credibility.

Degrees, advanced degrees, certifications, and licenses all fall within the traditional forms of credibility, and of course should be included within the body of your outreach. However, anyone who has taken the time and effort to pursue any of these traditional means of establishing credibility, but for whatever reason did not or has not completed the full requirements to be awarded the final degree, should still incorporate these efforts within the body.

Let's pick up with Jane Marie Doe again as she presents her credentials, and also incorporates those elements that she feels can establish her as "unique" in the eyes of the decision maker.

Example body verbiage & its elements

"Although I hold an advanced degree in Bio Chemistry, it is my 25 years of experience working directly with children afflicted with Autism, Muscular Dystrophy, and a plethora of other special needs, that I feel has provided me the level of passion I now maintain and incorporate in my extensive work with clients in every arena. My love for the volunteer work I do within my community contributes immensely to the current level of joy I experience in my own day-to-day life."

In this section, Jane successfully presented her formal education and its area of application, but also provided the decision maker with yet another glimpse into the personal side of her life by siting an example of her "give back" attitude and how it contributes to her life. These small and oftentimes overlooked approaches can do much in creating a template of likeability, the element that could very well whisper to the decision maker that YES, I like this person!

If the decision maker has a personal connection in any way to either Autism, MD, special needs of children, or volunteerism…the way Jane has incorporated these "life truths" within her body could do much in the relationship development between the decision maker and herself. The manner in which Jane dropped these breadcrumbs, all of which serve as possible *likeability connectors*, could very well be the breadcrumbs that eventually get her hired.

The Conclusion

So now that Jane has the ball rolling in her favor, what should she do next? We now approach the intersection where the decision maker will begin looking for *your solution to their problem/challenge*, the reason that has brought you both together in the first place. I have heard this referred to as the "mess to success" portion of the contemplation stage, this is where you must cut to the chase and present and convince the decision maker that you have EXACTLY what they need to achieve their objective in bringing in a speaker. As easy as this may sound, it is oftentimes where many speakers drop the ball or abandon ship all together. The solution element of any message must be clear and concise, it can never leave the decision maker still asking questions regarding how it is you intend to fix their problem or even the process you propose to utilize in doing so.

Let's look at how Jane accomplishes this task.

Example conclusion verbiage & its elements

"In today's society, it is not uncommon for the most 'together' person to, at some point, find themselves in need of additional tools to assist in navigating through the everchanging and uncharted waters of life. My program, 'The 5 keys to a more fulfilling everything' provides an easy to understand method of achieving breakthroughs in nearly all areas of life. Our success stories range

from the corporate CEO to the suburban housewife. 5 EASY KEYS… promises to do for most what they have not been able to do for themselves, to once and for all provide what has previously been missing. Those tools which when used properly, will lead them to the purpose filled life they have always desired."

Jane's first task was to clearly define a potential PROBLEM/CHALLENGE that she feels the decision maker is looking to repair. Jane creates yet another layer of trust by placing the decision maker at ease with her statement "**…it is not uncommon…**". This approach clearly speaks to the fact that this is nothing new to Jane, she deals with this very issue all the time in her work. I would imagine if I were the decision maker, that this is the point where I would finally sigh a breath of relief. This is where I would realize what is most likely the most vital component besides trust in the decision-making process, and that is – Jane gets it! Jane UNDERSTANDS my problem.

The next thing that Jane does to guide the decision maker along is to make the decision maker comfortable with the idea that the problem/challenge is something that she has a solution for, a solution that has a proven track record that covers a broad spectrum of lifestyles.

Jane further builds another layer of trust in the relationship simply by using the term "**promises**" in lieu of "**guarantees**". This may seem small and inconsequential, but the word *promises* seems more like a "personal" commitment than the word *guarantees* does. It simply again convinces the decision maker that they personally "like" Jane, but more importantly…they trust her.

Jane rounds out this section with a subtle call-to-action which also serves as a disclaimer of sorts; "…**those tools which when used properly**…". Jane has in this brief passage not only let herself off the hook in as far as her saying that this program works 100% of the time, but also introduces the fact that nothing she contributes can help if the program is not applied.

Provided Jane has included the additional tools of the trade within her presentation package, chances are that if she and the decision maker agree that this is a good fit…at a minimum, the decision maker will now feel the need and desire to delve even deeper into who Jane is and what it is she does.

When all is said and done, if conveyed with authenticity and passion, your initial outreach no matter which platform you utilize…should serve you well in the dropping of successful breadcrumbs.

There is an obligation, a duty for each of us that hold the honorable status of "Speaker", to not only represent ourselves and our message in the highest regard, but to also do whatever we can to assist the decision maker/meeting planner along the road of discovery.

There are millions of messages that never get the opportunity to be shared, to be heard, to live their intended purpose. Our heartfelt desire is for your message to never fall into that category.

By taking the time to artfully master the craft of successfully "DROPPING THE BREADCRUMBS", there is no doubt that your message will find its mark, your story will be told, and your purpose will continue to change the lives of the masses.

Utilizing the tools here will lead to successfully booking more speaking gigs.

Sharing Your Message: The "How" is in the Healing

If you remember, back in chapter 5... I made the statement that I had once asked myself (and the Creator); "Why would anyone want to listen to me?" I even went as far as stating that I considered the idea of sharing my story to help others as *ludicrous*.

I now believe that I better understand why the question of my ever having anything worthy of saying was so very challenging for me to comprehend. I now understand that the primary reason it was so very difficult for me to incorporate the sharing of my message with the world within my process, was since I had not yet reached the point wherein

I understood that it would not be simply a sharing of the many traumatic episodes I had lived to that point, since it would be the layers of healing I had experienced.

Healing, let's just take a moment and consider the true ramifications of what this word truly means. Webster's dictionary defines healing as; "The process of making or becoming *sound** or healthy again." When I process the complete definition of what healing means now in my life,

I find myself literally staring at the word "sound" found within the definition. I don't know about you, but I personally don't believe that I have ever included the term "sound" within my perception of what true healing represents. Sure, I have always understood healing to mean the process of something repairing itself, or something becoming whole again…returning to the state it originally was, but never have I ever included the idea of something becoming "sound" within my healing mindset.

For me, when I think of something being sound; I think of solid, complete, or whole. It was not until I began to understand the true definition of healing that I was able to see that although I was indeed making progress (at least in my eyes) in moving past certain difficult situations from my past, I was in no way becoming a more sound being, I was merely "going through situations" and not truly "growing through situations".

The healing of our bodies is quite different than the healing of our minds, our spirits. Whereas we can apply ointments, take prescribed or over-the-counter medications to promote the healing of bodily aliments, it is nowhere near as simplistic when it comes to the healing of our spirits from those "near death" emotional experiences we encounter along life's highway.

*Emphasis mine
I will never forget when I was embarking upon what must have been the third or fourth journey with severe depression within my early adulthood, I attempted for the first time to obtain some outside professional help by visiting a psychiatrist. I entered the doctor's office and watched him intently as he hurriedly jotted what I assumed were case notes for the patient I passed on

my way into his office. "Please have a seat" the psychiatrist said; all without even looking up to acknowledge me. I remember how horribly nervous I was about sharing my innermost secreted demons with a stranger, and the fact that already my presence felt like an unwelcomed intrusion did not help matters. After only sharing my story for no more than 10 minutes or so, the psychiatrist finally glanced up and contacted me saying; "Here, take this prescription, get it filled and make an appointment for a follow-up visit in 90 days."

I was stunned, especially since I had not even noticed that he had transitioned from writing in his binder notebook to a prescription pad, and I quickly asked as I took the prescription from his hand; "What's this and what's it for?" "It's Lithium", the doctor stated; "…and it's to help with your depression." When I asked how long I could expect to be taking this medication (which I knew nothing about, including any potential side effects), I nearly fell from my seat when I was forced to process the response of; "for life!"

I promptly threw the prescription back on the doctors' desk and exited his office, and this time it was I who offered no eye contact! As I drove away from my appointment that day, I shall never forget how utterly alone and afraid I felt. I felt as if what little hope I maintained that I could one day be free of the enormous pain and regret I then embraced with all my might, had just been snatched from within my reach…forever! It felt as if I had just received news that I was afflicted with some terminal disease and that time for me was at best, running out…and quickly.

Here is where that spontaneous decision gets sticky, although it is obvious to me now that my decision to avoid a lifetime of prescription medications in order to deal with my trauma of the past was a wise choice; I still nonetheless was taking a huge misstep in life by doing so.

After several weeks of attempting to locate an alternative route to prescription medications all with zero positive results, I found myself sinking deeper and deeper into my depression. Finally, the day came when I turned the volume of the negative voice within me up to the maximum level and began listening to the plan that sounded at the time like my only option available.

This option was nearly the undoing of my purpose in life, the extinguishing of my passion for life, and my path to exiting this world leaving a legacy of shame and heartbreak. I decided to self-medicate and just like that, virtually overnight…I dove head first within an addiction to street drugs that would drag me spirit first over the rockiest terrain for the next 14 years. Looking back in retrospect, it is now of course much easier for me to understand, clearer for me to see *and* share with others just what a potentially fatal decision this truly was, my self-medicating to avoid the pain, but nonetheless does not in any way discount how I was feeling at the time.

When feeling as if we have gone as far as one can go, have done all that one can do…the search for freedom from pain can lead to some very unhealthy decisions, which for various reasons will make all the sense in the world at the time. The healing of emotional wounds is in my opinion the most difficult healing process of all to initiate. After all, unlike a physical wound which is either apparent to the naked eye or if internal, obvious due to warning signals that something is just not right...our emotional wounds are extremely difficult to access, let alone diagnose.

Had I been aware at the time of the actual definition of healing, and had I considered whether or not my decision to self-medicate would eventually led me to a form of healing based in "soundness of spirit", things just may have taken a turn for the better within my life, but that was not to be my journey.

When growing our messages for the masses, it is imperative from day one that we seek out whatever courage is necessary to "cut and paste" those life lessons which we have already mastered, those hard times that we have already lived through. The cutting and pasting of those most difficult seasons of one's life is not as easy as many would have you believe, it requires a level of self-honesty that many survivors of trauma are not aware even exists. For many years I was the sole saboteur of my own emotional healing, simply due to my inability to forgive the past and others from the past, as well as my insistence on continuing to blame everything and everyone else for whatever I was unhappy or uncomfortable with within my life.

Just as a physical wound requires some form of a dressing to protect the wound from unwanted bacteria and germs, so does the human spirit. Unfortunately, most of us reach for denial, self-blame, regret, and retaliation to dress our emotional wounds with, and of course these remedies eventually prove themselves to not be remedies at all, since the spirit-eating, dream-killing, mass weapons of destructions they truly are.

So how *does* one know which emotional medicine cabinet to reach within when so desperately in need of an emotional bandage? Well the first thing you should understand is that emotional wounds require stages of healing in the same manner as burns to our skin. Severe burns to the human skin are not capable of healing simply by forming a blister which contains healing fluids, as minor burns can. Severe burns cause damage in varying degrees which represent the layers of skin that were affected during the injury, they require a thorough cleaning first to assure that the wound does not become infected, and in many cases require a daily scrubbing process that is considered one of the most painful processes the human body can endure.

The healing process for burns to the human body can take often months and months to heal, and even after the skin has healed there is pain, discomfort and excruciating itching that can last for years and in some cases…for life. Burn victims upon physical healing must then decide how they plan on dealing with the aftermath of their injuries, for some this means skin grafting or perhaps plastic surgery. There is also the matter of disfiguring that burn victims must deal with, and the realization of what a truly cruel and judgmental world we live in, and the after effects just go on and on.

The healing of emotional injuries is very similar to what I have just described regarding the healing of burns to the human body; there will be varying degrees of injury, some of our injuries will heal over with the assistance of a simple blister and the healing fluids held within, others will be much more painful, burn through many additional layers of our emotional skin, require many months or perhaps years of healing. There will be the obvious outward scaring, but in many cases even deeper scars that only you will see. And yes…we too, just as burn victims must, will find that we must now fight even harder to understand and survive within a world that can be cruel and judgmental of our scars.

My advice to you is thus, remember…there is a reason we are taught throughout life to develop a "thick skin" wherein it pertains to our emotions. Our emotional skin thickens with each battle we conquer, with each time we are burned by life or those within our lives, with each bandage changing we endure, and with each battle scar we wear with pride.

To grow through the trials and hardships that we must all endure while on our journey toward sharing our messages with the masses, we must be willing and accepting of the many challenges that offer up the questions which derail and dismantle so many dreams for so many people.

Why me?
When will my turn come?
What will my story be?
Where to now?

And then there is the question of all questions… **How** can I change the world for better?

How can I share my message with the masses…?

Begin today the changing of the bandages from having been burned in life, begin moving through the pain of having been burned by others and false opportunities, begin by simply asking yourself;

"**How** badly do I want to make a difference in this world?"

Ask **how** and there will always be only one answer;

How far am I willing to go to reach my healing? For the "**How**" is **in** the healing, I promise you that!

Chapter 9: Tools of the Trade – It's Show Time!

Now that you have reached this point, you should have a good understanding of how to position yourself and get speaking gigs booked. With that foundation in place, it's time to learn how to present like a pro!

This chapter covers everything from preparation/set-up of your presentation to follow-through with your audience to ensure that your presentation is not only remarkable, but unforgettable. While authentically serving your audience, having the stage is also an opportunity to grow your business (in a non-pitchy manner) and advance your branding as a sought-after speaker.

Technology Tips for Speakers

As a professional speaker, it is in your best interest to learn how to leverage technology. This will facilitate you getting attention, engaging your audience, closing more deals, and ultimately growing your business and sharing your message.

As part of the preparation for any speaking engagement, to the fully extent possible, make sure you can confidently walk in knowing how the show will run. Speak with your contact in advance and arrive with the tools that all speakers should have.

To start with, here is a list of what I use and recommend for my clients. Now, if you are just starting out, this list will be more of a wish list and something you can acquire over time. At a minimum, you really need a laptop, a clicker, and a Keynote Presentation in PowerPoint.

Tech Toolbox:

- **Tumi Backpack**

Tumi backpacks are durable and last a long time. I prefer the Tumi Alpha 2 T-Pass Business Class Brief Pack, but all of them are great.

- **2 Laptops**

1 laptop is generally enough. If you want to have a backup, Dell and MacBook Pro are great options.

- **iPad Pro**

This can be used as a backup. In addition, you can use it to draw and project it on a screen. You can draw notes and it is really a perfect note taking device.

- **PowerPoint & Keynote**

A professional presentation is extremely important.

- **Clicker**

For moving through your presentation, a clicker is a must. They are economical and you can get one from Amazon. I prefer Kensington Remote.

- **"Grid-It" with Cables by Cocoon**

This is used to organize your extra headphones, USB, USB drives, and everything you'd ever need cable-wise. At about $15, it's an incredible value and you can purchase on Amazon.

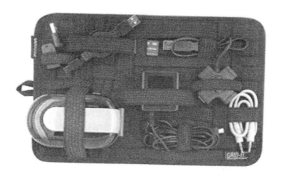

- **Video Adapters**

It is wise to carry your own adapter if you will be using your laptop for your presentation. This helps ensure you have what you need to have things run smoothly. Make sure you label all your equipment and using a Sharpie is an easy option.

- **Order Forms**

Always have all order forms saved on Dropbox or another easily accessible medium. You should be able to get from anywhere at any time.

- **Lavalier Microphone**

Make sure you record high quality audio when taking an interview and look good when giving a presentation – use a lavalier microphone like Sennheiser or Sony.

- **Projector**

You may save a lot of money having your own projector instead of renting at a venue. DLP Projectors are very bright.

- **Box of Books**

Books can be a great giveaway. If you're able to do a presentation on stage, you may tell them you have a limited number of books you give away. At the end of the presentation, all these people can line up to get a signed copy and you can show your order forms while they wait.

PowerPoint Slide Rules

When it comes to preparation for a venue, assume the worst. Assume that every single person in the room elderly with bad eyesight, that the lighting will be poor, and that the technology will be dated. Why prepare for this? Because all these things can and do happen.

As such, with your presentation, make sure that your slides have minimal text. Be clear and concise with what the audience is seeing and rely on your voice to provide greater detail. Relevant pictures as an effective communication tool are excellent.

At the end, it is fine to share your contact information on a slide, but don't expect that to be what continues the relationship you have started. It is ALWAYS better to get your audience members' contact information – "Text into", "Sign-up for…." If you haven't incorporated lead capture technology yet, make sure you are asking people for their business cards as you are conversing after your presentation.

Presentation Mastery

When you walk onto that stage, you want to own that stage. Own that room. You're in charge. Because, think about it; when the speaker's in charge, do you feel good as an audience member, that like, "Ah this is going to be good." Think about this, when you hear someone walk up and they're like, "Okay, boom, boom, boom. Hi, I'm really nervous right now." What just happened to you? You and all your fellow audience members checked out.

All of us want to be the speaker that people are immediately engaged with and feel confident that we are a valuable use of their time. So, let's go through some of the elements that effectively serve our audience and seamlessly continue our conversation after the presentation ends.

An ideal presentation is where the speaking and the training and the selling are very seamless, and it isn't like this weird ugly transition that just feels awkward.

During my presentations, I am not pitching anything, but I am seeding throughout the entire presentation. In other words, the way we do this, it feels comfortable. It's like a normal part of the discussion and it's not this odd pitchy thing. It's because this part of it was set up right as you move into the close, where everything is great. What I'm going to do is give you an outline for a great talk, but I'm going to do more than that.

As we move into this we'll be talking about speaking almost the entire time, but remember you can use this outline for webinars, webcasts. You can use it for teleseminars. If you're doing a video sales letter, this format will work great for that shoot. You could even use it as the outline for your book.

The first thing you're going to do is grab attention. Our job is to engage people so much within the first minutes that they decide to stay, listen to you speaking and that they can't wait to hear what you must say. So, what can you do in the first five minutes of your talk to engage your audience?

- **Start with a story**. A relevant story is one of the best ways to help your listeners get immersed in the moment and compelled to stay and hear the end of the story. You can craft the lesson of your story to make any point you want, as long it connects to your content and is truthful.

- **Start with a question**. Like a story, starting with a question immediately engages listeners and puts them in the moment. A question is also a great way to transition into a story—like the question that I'd used to open the training. "What do you do if you only have 5 seconds to live?"

Second thing you're going to do is explain "Who You Are, and Why People Should Listen to You".

Here, your objective is to prove why you are a credible source on this topic. Though it seems counterintuitive since you want to establish yourself as an expert, as an authority you need to bring yourself down to the audience's level.

What does that mean? When you're standing on stage, there is already an inherent distance between you and your audience. Whether you realize it or not, your status suddenly seems unattainable. Your job is to make yourself real, humanize yourself. Show pictures of yourself as a child, talk about your background, and give people points of connection to you and your story. Bring yourself down a little, in a playful way "I failed third grade" and then immediately boost your credibility by showing how far you've come.

Grab attention and then tell your story. This story can be same as first story or can be different. Either Way, the model of the story is called mess to success. It's always a story of how you were kind of screwed up and how you fixed your problem with the solution that you're going to provide for them.

Make sure that you still cover all of your accomplishments and what makes you a credible expert worthy of their trust and attention. Emphasize the tools and strategies you used to achieve the success, since those are what you'll be presenting to your audience. The function of bringing yourself down is making people think, "If he/she can do it, I can do it too."

The third thing that you're going to do is Explain the What and the Why, Not the How.

When covering your talking points, teach the what, the why, but not the how. Similar to walking through your services in a 1:1 presentation, your focus here is to emphasize the benefits, but not the technical details or the features. That said, don't hesitate to list all that's necessary to complete the strategies you outline, so that listeners feel that it is something they couldn't do on their own.

Remember, when you get to the close of your presentation, you will cover all the services and most important tasks you listed in this part of your presentation. Set it up in a way that the audience feels a sigh of relief when they hear that you can take care of all of those things. You can even incorporate a slide that checks each of the elements you listed one by one, so the audience gets a visual representation of how comprehensive your services are.

The fourth thing that you're going to do is incorporate Seeding. Seeding is providing great content in such a way that the audience wants to continue to learn from you or work with you more.

The body of your presentation is the right time to give a call to action to get audience's contact information. While explaining one of the points, make an example where you explain that you understand it may be confusing, and ask if a strategy session with you would be helpful. Then, ask for their business cards.

Here's where you can insert the single phrase "One of the things I do with my private coaching/consulting clients is YOU ___. Help the listeners to imagine and visualize working with you.

There are a few elements that should be considered in every presentation:

1. Make a list of all the things you're going to deliver to the audience. Generally, this list will make the teaching points of the presentation and should incorporate the benefits these items and you offer them. (10 is a common amount)

2. Make a list of Common Myths that you are going to debunk. This actually helps the audience members overcome objections without having to verbalize them. Think about what people may object to and how to counter these concerns. From the myths, explain why they aren't accurate and give compelling examples of this.

   - "Too expensive"
   - "I don't need help"
   - "I've tried this before"
   - Etc.

3. Calls to Action – Be casual about it, as if it is normal part of the conversation you are having… "By the way, I know this is a lot of information in a short amount of time. Obviously, this isn't the venue to tailor all this specifically to everyone, but I am happy to help you get more clarity. If it would be helpful to you, introduce yourself and hand me your

business card. We can schedule 30 minutes to connect in the next week."

More general Calls to Action include:

- Call me
- Email me
- Schedule a consultation
- Go to mywebsite.com
- Meet me at the back of the room

Transition to Close

"Now" is the word that you can use to do the first step, which is called the transition. You have to go from your talk into your close. As you transition, one of the most important things is congruence. You need to keep the same thing going through. How will you be congruent? Practice it. Take yourself connected to the offer in such a way that you feel like it's the best thing for them because it is.

Mastering the transition from teaching to selling has as much to do with what you say as it does with how you say it. They key is to practice transitioning into the close, and then to practice your close before you practice the rest of the presentation. It's important to be comfortable with the final part of the pitch.

First, watch your body language and make sure that you maintain the same open, honest, conversational style. Your audience will be able to sense a change.

Also, don't suddenly change your pace, the way you're standing, or how you're interacting with your audience and do not hide behind your podium and read from a sheet. Stay engaged, stay mobile, and keep your energy high.

At the end always say "When": "When we work to together, that's how you benefit..., that's what happens..."

Conclusion

We started our journey together by working on your mindset. When you open your mind, and get out of your own way, great things start happening in your life.

Our goal was to help you get your message out to the world and make sure you're not the best kept secret around. To accomplish this, you must understand your market, message and the media that's going to be used to make it effective.

Positioning yourself as an expert in your field makes it easier for you to stand out and be noticed. Event planners are looking at your social media, video's and your followers in their decision-making process. The clearer your message is and the more targeted audience you have will create demand for your services.

Making sure your follow-up process is flawless will help project your professionalism and you will win more paid opportunities.

Showing up with the right equipment and a well-organized presentation will leave a positive impression for the audience and event planners. This will not only lead to them recommending you, but also engage them to continue the conversation and interact with you long after the presentation is over. You are positioned to leave a legacy that will last forever!

Other Books by Barry

All Seven of Barry's books reached the Amazon #1 Best Seller list, the Amazon International Best Seller

The Money is in Your Message

Create and Monetize your Message

Digital to Dollars
How to Get Clients Fast and Achieve Unstoppable Growth!

7 New Marketing Rules

Success Junkie:
12 Principles for Winning the Life of your Dreams

Barry Currently Speaks on...

- CREATING YOUR MESSAGE

- HOW TO CREATE INCOME STREAMS THAT MAKE YOU MONEY WHILE YOU SLEEP

- CUTTING EDGE MARKETING STRATEGY

- BOOK CREATION AND MARKETING FOR AUTHORS, EXPERTS, SPEAKERS AND CONSULTANTS

- HOW TO GET CLIENTS FAST

- HOW TO GET SPEAKING GIGS FAST

- CREATING CELEBRITY

- MARKETING AUTOMATION

- LEAD GENERATION

- DREAMING BIG

Other Books by Loren

Coming soon!!!

Loren Currently Speaks on...

- THE RIPPLE EFFECT
- WRITING YOUR NEVER-ENDING STORY
- THE ART OF BUILDING YOUR TEAM FROM THE INSIDE OUT
- BUILDING TRUST: FROM ORGANIZATIONAL TO CUSTOMER BASE
- PERSONAL DEVELOPMENT: THE KEY TO EVERYTHING ELSE!
- CUSTOMER SERVICE SO GOOD, YOUR GRANDMA WILL BE TALKING ABOUT IT!
- CREATING AN IMPACT ON THE WORLD THAT LASTS FOREVER
- BELIEVING IN YOURSELF WHEN NO ONE ELSE CAN
- BREAKING THE TWO STEPS FORWARD, THREE STEPS BACK CYCLE
- BUILDING A FUTURE THAT MANY ONLY DREAM ABOUT
- YOUR RESPONSIBILITY TO THE RIPPLE EFFECT
- HOW TO TAKE THE FIGHT OUT OF BULLYING
- HOW TO LIVE PURPOSE DRIVEN MOMENTS
- FOSTER CARE/ADOPTION

Congratulations!

It is time to first celebrate your victory. You created a goal of finishing this book, and now you have accomplished it. It is very important to take time, even if it can only be a moment, to celebrate your victories.

Recognize that you are one step closer to reaching your Vision. Know that we are proud of your success and very grateful that you took the time to learn and consider how you are going to implement our teachings.

Your next step is to nurture these lessons and then take massive action!

"Inaction breeds doubt and fear. Action breeds confidence and courage. If you want to conquer fear, do not sit home and think about it. Go out and get busy"

~ Dale Carnegie

To your success!!!!

Barry and Loren